# About Happier...

This book is not airport flotsam, but a serious, practical attempt to address the ennui of affluence... Recommended most strongly to all who are serious about the question, "what constitutes a worthwhile and happy life?"
**Management Today**

In Happier, Harvard University's Tal Ben-Shahar puts a new spin on positive psychology with the belief that you can transform not only yourself but your partner, too, just by making behavioural changes that can alter how you interact!
**Zest**

Manageable, well researched and very accessible... Its no-nonsense approach and positive stance make for an inspirational read
**Kindred Spirit**

Ben Shahar's ideas are well-sourced in academic theory and, at the same time, presented in a straightforward and entirely practical way. The result is this rare accomplishment – a wonderfully readable and simple presentation of a complex set of ideas which serve as an invaluable guide to enhancing the lives of its readers.
**Rabbi Andrew Savage Ma (Oxon), Aish UK Campus Rabbi, Oxford and Cambridge Universities**

Happier gives much thought to the idea of reconciling happiness and ambition. Most people live under the illusion that, if they achieve something they will be happy. "that is just not the case" says Tal Ben Shahar. "It's the steps along the way that are important".
**Red**

In Happier, Tal Ben Shahar explains that "to turn the potential for happiness into a reality, we first need to realize that the possibility exists."
**The Times**

"Count your blessings" is the advice of Tal Ben Shahar, a Harvard University psychologist, who has written the latest self-help book detailing some simple ways to make your life happier.
**Daily Mail**

Happier is inspiring, uplifting and readable ... one of those rare self-help books that really could change your life.
**www.new-classics.co.uk**

An uplifting and life-changing book ... it will help you achieve more pleasure and meaning in your life.
**sixtyplussurfers.co.uk**

This engrossing, fascinating blueprint for bliss [provides] the information and tools for finding your inner fun – today, every day.
**Daily Record**

This might just work! ... There's a lot more substance to this book than others on the market. Warm and genuine.
**Relentlesslypositive.com**

Tal Ben-Shahar's work has not only motivated me to reshape the way in which I teach my psychology students, but I have seen at first hand how his book Happier has enabled them to re-evaluate their own personal perspectives and future plans—and to feel that they are living happier lives as a direct consequence!
**Dr. Deborah Jima-Otero CPsychol AFBPsS, Senior Lecturer and Personal Coach, The Newcastle Centre for Positive Living, Northumbria University**

Tal Ben Shahar is a lecturer in positive psychology and blends theories from science, self-help and spiritual learning into useful daily tips. His advice includes simplifying your life by asking yourself "what can I say no to?"
**Spirit and Destiny**

The message here is: hurry up and slow down!
**Accounting & Business**

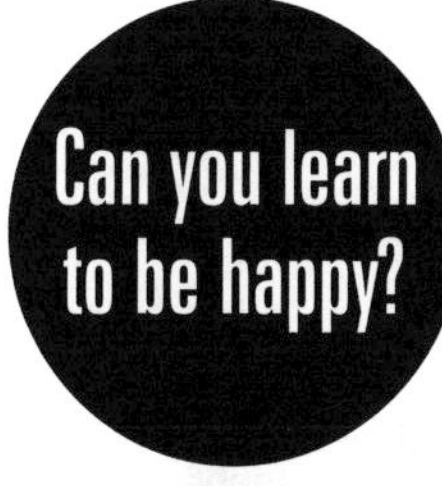


# HAPPIER

*TAL BEN-SHAHAR, Ph.D.*

New York Chicago San Francisco Lisbon London Madrid Mexico City
Milan New Delhi San Juan Seoul Singapore Sydney Toronto

Happier:
Can you learn to be happy?

Tal Ben-Shahar

ISBN 13: 978-0-07-712324-6
ISBN 10: 0-07-712324-7

Published by:
McGraw-Hill Publishing Company
Shoppenhangers Road, Maidenhead, Berkshire, England, SL6 2QL
Telephone: 44 (0) 1628 502500
Fax: 44 (0) 1628 770224
Website: www.mcgraw-hill.co.uk

**British Library Cataloguing in Publication Data**
A catalogue record of this book is available from the British Library.





**Printed in Great Britain by Bell and Bain Ltd, Glasgow.**



The McGraw·Hill Companies

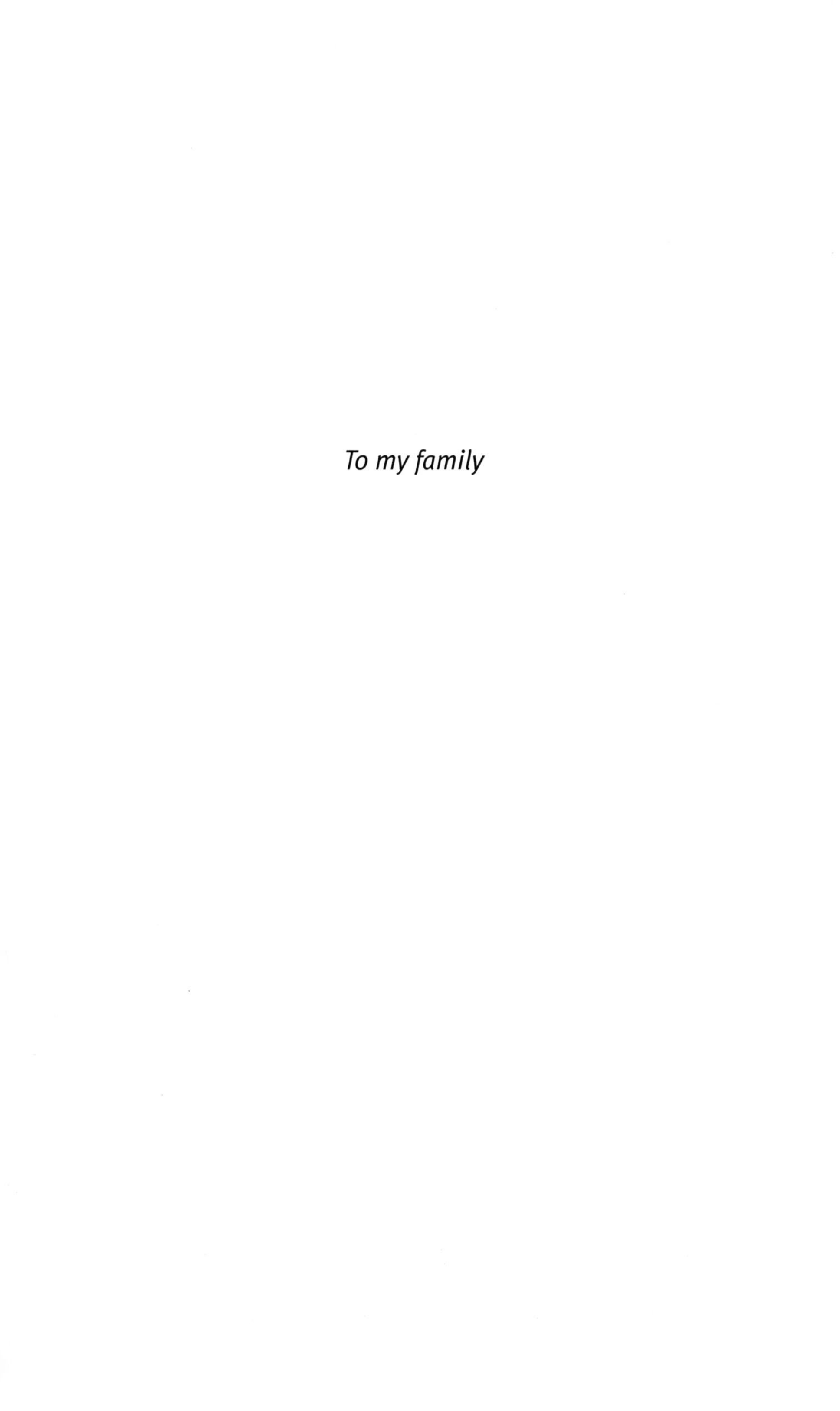

*To my family*

# Contents

# Preface

**We all live with the objective of being happy; our lives are all different and yet the same.**

—*Anne Frank*

I first taught a positive psychology seminar at Harvard in 2002. Eight students signed up; two dropped out. In class each week, we explored what I believed to be *the question of questions*: how can we help ourselves and others—individuals, communities, and society—become happier? We read academic journal articles, tested ideas, shared personal stories, experienced frustration as well as delight, and, by the end of the year, emerged with a clearer understanding of what psychology can teach us about leading happier, more fulfilling lives.

The following year the class went public, in a manner of speaking. My mentor Philip Stone, who first introduced me to the field and was also the first professor to teach positive psychology at Harvard, encouraged me to offer a lecture course on the topic. Three hundred eighty students signed up. In their year-end evaluations, more than 20 percent noted that "the course improves the quality of one's life." The next time I offered the course, 855 students enrolled, making it the largest class at the university.

William James, who over a century ago founded American psychology, kept me on track by reminding me to remain practical and seek "truth's cash-value in experiential terms." The cash-value that I primarily sought for the students was not in hard currency or the currency of success and accolades but rather in what I've come to call the ultimate currency, the end toward which all other ends lead: happiness.

This was not merely a class on the theory of "the good life." Students, beyond reading articles and learning about the research in the field, were asked to apply the material. They wrote papers in which they grappled with their fears and reflected on their strengths, set ambitious goals for the week and for the coming decade; they were encouraged to take risks and find their stretch zone (the healthy median between their comfort and panic zones).

Personally, I was not always able to find that healthy median. As a shy introvert, I felt fairly comfortable the first time I taught the class with six students. Lecturing in front of close to four hundred students the following year, however, was certainly a stretch for me. When the class more than doubled in the third year, I was firmly in the panic zone—especially once students' parents, a handful of grandparents, and then the media started to show up.

Since the day that the *Harvard Crimson* and then the *Boston Globe* reported on the popularity of the class, the deluge of questions hasn't stopped. People are sensing—have been sensing for a while—that we are in the midst of some sort of revolution, and they are not sure why. How can you explain the demand for positive psychology at Harvard and on other college campuses? Why this growing interest in the study of happiness, in elementary and high schools, as well as among the adult population? Is it because people are more depressed today? Is it something about a twenty-first-century education or our Western way of life?

In fact, the study of happiness is unique neither to our hemisphere nor to our postmodern age. People everywhere, and always, have sought the key to happiness. Plato institutionalized the study of the good life in his Academy, while his star student, Aristotle, opened the competing Lyceum to promote his own take on flourishing. More than a century earlier, and on another continent, Confucius walked from village to village to share his prescription for fulfillment. No great religion or comprehensive philosophical system is indifferent to the question of happiness, whether in this world or in the afterlife. More recently, self-help gurus have occupied large parts of bookstores and conference centers around the world—from India to Indiana, from Jerusalem to Jeddah.

But while interest in, and study of, the good life transcends time and place, there are some unique aspects in our age that help explain the high demand for positive psychology. In the United States, rates of depression are ten times higher today than they were in the 1960s, and the average age for the onset of depression is fourteen and a half compared to twenty-nine and a half in 1960. A study conducted in American colleges tells us that nearly 45 percent of students were "so depressed that they had difficulty functioning." Other countries are following in the footsteps of the United States. In 1957, 52 percent in Britain said that they were very happy, compared to 36 percent in 2005—despite the fact that the British have tripled their wealth over the last half century. With the rapid growth in the Chinese economy comes a rapid growth in the number of adults and children who experience anxiety and depression. According to the Chinese Health Ministry, "The mental health status of our country's children and youths is indeed worrying."

While levels of material prosperity are on the rise, so are levels of depression. Even though our generation—in most Western countries as well as in an increasing number of places in the East—is wealthier than previous generations, we are not happier for it. A leading scholar in the field of positive psychology, Mihaly Csikszentmihalyi, asks a simple question with a complex answer: "If we are so rich, why aren't we happy?"

As long as people believed that their basic material needs had to be met in order for them to lead a fulfilling life, it was easy to explain away unhappiness. But now, with the basic needs of many having been met, there is no longer a ready-made justification for discontent. More and more people are looking to resolve the paradox—that money seems to have bought us unhappiness—and they are turning to positive psychology for help.

## Why Positive Psychology?

Positive psychology—generally referred to as "the scientific study of optimal human functioning"[1]—was officially launched as a field of study in 1998 by Martin Seligman, president of the American Psychological Association. Until that year, the study of happiness—of enhancing the quality of our lives—had largely been dominated by pop psychology. In the multitude of self-help seminars and books, there is much fun and charisma, and yet many (though far from all) offer little substance. They promise five easy steps to happiness, the three secrets of success, and four ways to find your perfect lover. These are usually empty promises, and over the years, people have become cynical about self-help.

On the other side we have academe, with writing and research that are substantive but that do not find their way into most households. As I see it, the role of positive psychology is to bridge the ivory tower and Main Street, the rigor of academe and the fun of the self-help movement. That, too, is the purpose of this book.

Many self-help books overpromise and underdeliver, because few of them are subjected to the test of the scientific method. In contrast, ideas that have appeared in academic journals and have passed the academic process from conception to publication usually have much more substance. While their authors are generally less grandiose, making fewer promises to fewer readers, these authors also tend to deliver on their promises.

And yet, because positive psychology bridges the ivory tower and Main Street, advice given by positive psychologists—whether in book form, in lectures, or on a website—can sometimes sound like the advice that self-help gurus offer. It is simple and accessible—like pop psychology is—but it is simple and accessible in a radically different way.

Supreme Court Justice Oliver Wendell Holmes remarked, "I would not give a fig for the simplicity on this side of complexity, but I would give my life for the simplicity on the other side of complexity." Holmes was interested in the simplicity that comes after searching and researching, deep reflection, and laborious testing—not in baseless platitudes and off-the-cuff assertions. Positive psychologists—by delving into the depth of a phenomenon—emerge on the other side of complexity with accessible ideas and practical theories, as well as simple techniques and tips that work. This is no easy feat. Foreshadowing Holmes, Leonardo da Vinci pointed out that "simplicity is the ultimate sophistication."

Concerned with distilling the essence of the good life, positive psychologists, alongside other social scientists and philosophers, have spent a great deal of time and effort attempting to reach the simplicity on the other side of complexity. Their ideas, some of which I describe in this book, can help you lead a happier, more fulfilled life. I know they can—they have done so for me.

## Using This Book

This book is intended to help you understand the nature of happiness; more than that, it is intended to help you become happier. But merely reading this book (or any other book for that matter) is unlikely to make that happen. I do not believe that there are shortcuts to meaningful change, and if this book is to have a real impact on your life, you have to treat it as a workbook. The work has to comprise both reflection and action.

Effortlessly glossing over the text is not enough; deep reflection is necessary. Toward that end, throughout the book, there are breaks in the text labeled "Time-In" (as opposed to "Time-Out"). These are intended to provide you with an opportunity, a reminder, to stop for a few minutes, to reflect on what you have just read, to look inside yourself. Without the breaks, without taking a time-in, most of the material in this book will likely remain abstract for you—and thus be soon forgotten.

In addition to the Time-Ins throughout the text, at the end of each chapter there are longer exercises intended to elicit reflection and action—to help you take the material to a deeper level. Some of the exercises will probably resonate with you more than others will; for example, keeping a journal may be easier for you than meditating. Start by doing the exercises that feel most natural to you, and, as they begin to help, gradually expand your repertoire by doing others. However, if any exercise in the book does not make you feel good, simply don't do it and move on to the next one. The exercises are all based on what I have found to be the best interventions that psychologists have to offer—and the more time you invest in doing them, the more likely you are to benefit from the book.

The book is divided into three sections. In Part 1, Chapters 1 through 5, I discuss what happiness is and the essential components of a happy life; in the second part, Chapters 6 through 8, I focus on putting these ideas into practice in education, in the workplace, and in relationships; the final part comprises seven meditations in which I offer some thoughts on the nature of happiness and on its place in our lives.

In Chapter 1, I begin by recounting the experience that launched my search for a better life. In the following chapter, I argue that happiness arises neither from simply satisfying immediate desires nor from the infinite delay of satisfaction. Our usual models for happiness—the hedonist who lives only for pleasure in the moment and the rat racer who postpones gratification for the purpose of attaining some future goal—do not work for most people, because they ignore our basic need for a sense of both present and future benefit.

In Chapter 3, I demonstrate why, in order to be happy, we need to find both meaning and pleasure—to have both a sense of purpose and the experience of positive emotions. In Chapter 4, I suggest that happiness, not money or prestige, should be regarded as the ultimate currency—the currency by which we take measure of our lives. I consider the relationship between material wealth and happiness and ask why so many people are in danger of emotional bankruptcy despite unprecedented levels of material wealth. Chapter 5 ties the ideas presented in this book to the existing psychological literature on goal setting.

In Chapter 6, I begin to apply the theory and ask why most students dislike school. I then examine ways in which educators—parents and teachers—can help students to be both happy and successful. I introduce two radically different approaches toward the process of learning: the drowning model and the lovemaking model. Chapter 7 questions the prevalent assumption that a trade-off between an intrinsic sense of fulfillment and extrinsic success at work is inevitable. I discuss the process by which we can identify work that we find meaningful and pleasurable and that we are good at. In Chapter 8, I look at one of the most significant elements of a happy life: relationships. I talk about what it really means to love and be loved unconditionally, why this kind of love is essential for a happy relationship, and how it can contribute to the experience of pleasure and meaning in other areas of our lives.

In the First Meditation of the final part of the book, I discuss the relationship between happiness, self-interest, and benevolence. In the Second Meditation I introduce the idea of happiness boosters—brief activities that provide both meaning and pleasure, and that can have an effect on our overall levels of well-being. In the Third Meditation, I challenge the idea that our level of happiness is predetermined by our genetic makeup or early experiences and that it cannot be changed. The Fourth Meditation identifies ways of overcoming some of the psychological barriers—those internal limitations that we impose upon ourselves and that stand in the way of living a fulfilling life. The Fifth Meditation provides a thought experiment that offers a point from which we can reflect upon, and find some answers to, the question of questions. The Sixth Meditation considers how our attempt to fit more and more activities into less and less time may be impeding the possibility of leading happier lives.

The final meditation is dedicated to the happiness revolution. I believe that if enough people recognize the true nature of happiness as the ultimate currency, we will witness society-wide abundance not only of happiness but also of goodness.

# Acknowledgments

I wrote this book with much help from friends, students, and teachers. When I first asked Kim Cooper for help with an early draft of this book, I expected a few minor recommendations before I could send it off to publishers. It was not to be. The hundreds of hours we subsequently spent working together on this book—arguing, discussing, sharing, laughing—have made writing this book the labor of happiness.

My special thanks to Shawn Achor, Warren Bennis, Johan Berman, Aletha Camille Bertelsen, Nathaniel Branden, Sandra Cha, I-Jin Chew, Leemore Dafny, Margot and Udi Eiran, Liat and Shai Feinberg, Dave Fish, Shayne Fitz-Coy, Jessica Glazer, Adam Grant, Richard Hackman, Nat Harrison, Anne Hwang, Ohad Kamin, Joe Kaplan, Ellen Langer, Maren Lau, Pat Lee, Brian Little, Joshua Margolis, Dan Markel, Bonnie Masland, Sasha Mattu, Jamie Miller, Mihnea Moldoveanu, Damian Moskovitz, Ronen Nakash, Jeff Perrotti, Josephine Pichanick, Samuel

Rascoff, Shannon Ringvelski, Amir and Ronit Rubin, Philip Stone, Moshe Talmon, and Pavel Vasilyev. The teaching staff and students in my positive psychology courses have provided me with an abundance of ideas—and an abundance of the ultimate currency.

In workshops, and in leisurely conversations, colleagues and friends from Tanker Pacific have played an important role in helping me develop the ideas in this book. My special thanks to Idan Ofer, Hugh Hung, Sam Norton, Anil Singh, Tadic Tongi, and Patricia Lim.

I am grateful to my agent, Rafe Sagalyn, for his patience, support, and encouragement. John Aherne, my editor at McGraw-Hill, believed in my work from the outset and helped make the publishing process so enjoyable.

I have been blessed with a large and close-knit family—they create a circle of happiness for me. To the Ben-Shahars, Ben-Poraths, Ben-Urs, Grobers, Kolodnys, Markses, Millers, Moseses, and Roses my gratitude for the countless hours we have spent—and will continue to spend—discussing and living the good life. To my grandparents, for living through the worst and exemplifying the best.

Many of the ideas in this book emerged from discussions with my brother and sister, Zeev and Ateret, two brilliant and insightful psychologists. Tami, my wife and helpmeet, patiently listened to my ideas when they were in the raw and then read and commented on everything that I wrote. Our children, David and Shirelle, patiently sat on my lap while my wife and I discussed the book (and once in a while turned around and smiled at me, reminding me what true bliss is). My parents provided me with the foundation from which I was able to write about—and, more important, to find—happiness.

# Part 1

# What Is HAPPINESS?

1

# The Question of Happiness

**In the middle of difficulty lies opportunity.**

*—Albert Einstein*

I was sixteen years old when I won the Israeli national squash championship. It was an event that brought the subject of happiness into sharp focus in my life.

I had always believed that winning the title would make me happy, would alleviate the emptiness I felt so much of the time. For the five years I had trained for the event I felt that something important was missing from my life—something that all of the miles run, the weights lifted, the self-motivating speeches playing and replaying in my mind were not providing. But I believed that it was only a matter of time before that "missing something" would find its way into my life. After all, it seemed clear to me that the mental and physical exertion were necessary to win the championship. Winning the championship was necessary for fulfillment. Fulfillment was necessary for happiness. That was the logic I operated under.

And, in fact, when I won the Israeli Nationals, I was ecstatic, happier than I had ever imagined myself being. Following the final match I went out with my family and friends, and we celebrated together. I was certain then that the belief that had carried me through the five years of preparation—that winning the title would make me happy—was justified; the hard work, the physical and emotional pain, had paid off.

After the night of celebration, I retired to my room. I sat on my bed and wanted to savor, for the last time before going to sleep, that feeling of supreme happiness. Suddenly, without warning, the bliss that came from having attained in real life what had for so long been my most cherished and exalted fantasy disappeared, and my feeling of emptiness returned. I was befuddled and afraid. The tears of joy shed only hours earlier turned to tears of pain and helplessness. For if I was not happy now, when everything seemed to have worked out perfectly, what prospects did I have of attaining lasting happiness?

I tried to convince myself that I was feeling the temporary low following an overwhelming high. But as the days and months unfolded, I did not feel happier; in fact, I was growing even more desolate as I began to see that simply substituting a new goal—winning the world championship, say—would not in itself lead me to happiness. There no longer seemed to be a series of logical steps for me to follow.

**TIME-IN** Reflect on a couple of personal experiences where reaching a certain milestone did not bring you the emotional payoff you expected.

I realized that I needed to think about happiness in different ways, to deepen or change my understanding of the nature of happiness. I became obsessed with the answer to a single question: how can I find lasting happiness? I pursued it fervently—I observed people who seemed happy and asked what it was that made them happy; I read everything I could find on the topic of happiness, from Aristotle to Confucius, from ancient philosophy to modern psychology, from academic research to self-help books.

To continue my exploration of the question of happiness in a more formal way, I decided to study philosophy and psychology in college. I met brilliant people who had dedicated themselves as writers, thinkers, artists, or teachers to understanding the "big questions." Learning to read a text closely and analytically, attending lectures on intrinsic motivation and on creativity, reading Plato on "the good" and Emerson on "the integrity of your own mind"—all of these provided me with new lenses through which my life and the lives of those around me came into clearer focus.

I was not alone in my unhappiness; many of my classmates seemed to be dispirited and stressed. And yet I was struck by how little time they dedicated to what I believed to be *the question of questions*. They spent their time pursuing high grades, athletic achievements, and prestigious jobs, but the pursuit—and attainment—of these goals failed to provide them with an experience of sustained well-being.

Although their specific goals changed when they left college (promotion at work replacing academic success, for instance), the essential pattern of their lives remained the same. So many people seemed to accept their poor emotional predicament as the inevitable price of success. Could it be, then, that Thoreau's observation that most people lead lives of "quiet desperation" was true? Even if it was, I refused to accept his dire assessment as a necessary fact of life and sought answers to the following questions: How can a person be both successful and happy? How can ambition and happiness be reconciled? Is it possible to defy the maxim of "no pain, no gain"?

In trying to answer these questions, I realized that I would first have to figure out what happiness is. Is it an emotion? Is it the same as pleasure? Is it the absence of pain? The experience of bliss? Words like *pleasure*, *bliss*, *ecstasy*, and *contentment* are often used interchangeably with the word *happiness*, but none of them describes precisely what I mean when I think about happiness. These emotions are fleeting, and while they are enjoyable and significant, they are not the measure—or the pillars—of happiness. We can experience sadness at times and still enjoy overall happiness.

While it was clear to me which words and definitions were inadequate, finding those that *could* capture the nature of happiness proved more difficult. We all talk about happiness and mostly know it when we experience it, but we lack a coherent definition that can help us identify its antecedents. The source of the word *happiness* is the Icelandic word *happ*, which means "luck" or "chance," the same source of the words *haphazard* and *happenstance*. I did not want to leave the experience of happiness to chance and therefore sought to define and understand it.

**TIME-IN** How would you define happiness? What does happiness mean to you?

I do not have the complete answer to the single question I posed at age sixteen—I suspect that I will never have it. Through my reading, research, observation, and reflection, I have discovered no secret formula, no "five easy steps to happiness." My objective in writing this book is to raise awareness of the general principles underlying a happy and fulfilling life.

These general principles are certainly not a panacea and, moreover, are not relevant for all people in all situations. I have mostly limited my focus to positive psychology and do not address many internal obstacles that prevent people from pursuing happiness, such as major depression or acute anxiety disorder. Nor are the ideas applicable for many of the external obstacles that come in the way of a flourishing life.

It is sometimes impossible for those living in a conflict area, under political oppression, or in extreme poverty to begin to apply the theory presented in the following pages. Following the loss of someone dear, it is exceedingly hard to concern oneself with the question of questions. Even in less severe situations—a disappointment, a difficult spell at work or within a relationship—it may be unhelpful to ask a person to focus on the pursuit of happiness. The best we may be able to do under some circumstances is to experience the negative emotions and allow them to take their natural course.

Some suffering is unavoidable in every life, and there are many external and internal barriers to the good life that cannot be overcome by reading a book. However, a better understanding of the nature of happiness—and, more important, applying certain ideas—can help most people in most situations become happier.

## From Happy to Happier

While writing this book or reading others' notions of happiness, when thinking about the good life and observing the behavior of those around me, I have often asked myself, "Am I happy?" Others have asked me a similar question. It took me a while to recognize that, while well meaning, this question is not helpful.

How do I determine whether I am happy or not? At what point do I become happy? Is there some universal standard of happiness, and, if there is, how do I identify it? Does it depend on my happiness relative to others, and, if it does, how do I gauge how happy other people are? There is no reliable way to answer these questions, and even if there were, I would not be happier for it.

"Am I happy?" is a closed question that suggests a binary approach to the pursuit of the good life: we are either happy or we are not. Happiness, according to this approach, is an end of a process, a finite and definable point that, when reached, signifies the termination of our pursuit. This point, however, does not exist, and clinging to the belief that it does will lead to dissatisfaction and frustration.

We can always be happier; no person experiences perfect bliss at all times and has nothing more to which he can aspire. Therefore, rather than asking myself whether I am happy or not, a more helpful question is, "How can I become happier?" This question acknowledges the nature of happiness and the fact that its pursuit is an ongoing process best represented by an infinite continuum, not by a finite point. I am happier today than I was five years ago, and I hope to be happier five years from now than I am today.

Rather than feeling despondent because we have not yet reached the point of perfect happiness, rather than squandering our energies trying to gauge how happy we are, we need to recognize that happiness is an unlimited resource and then focus on ways in which we can attain more of it. Becoming happier is a lifelong pursuit.

## EXERCISES

### Creating Rituals

We all know that change is hard. Much research suggests that learning new tricks, adopting new behaviors, or breaking old habits may be harder than we even realize and that most attempts at change, whether by individuals or organizations, fail.[1] It turns out that self-discipline is usually insufficient when it comes to fulfilling our commitments, even those we know are good for us—which is why most New Year's resolutions fail.

In their book *The Power of Full Engagement*, Jim Loehr and Tony Schwartz provide a different way of thinking about change: they suggest that instead of focusing on cultivating *self-discipline* as a means toward change, we need to introduce *rituals*. According to Loehr and Schwartz, "Building rituals requires defining very precise behaviors and performing them at very specific times—motivated by deeply held values."

Initiating a ritual is often difficult, but maintaining it is relatively easy. Top athletes have rituals: they know that at specific hours during each day they are on the field, after which they are in the gym, and then they stretch.[2] For most of us, brushing our teeth at least twice a day is a ritual and therefore does not require special powers of discipline. We need to take the same approach toward any change we want to introduce.

For athletes, being a top performer is a deeply held value, and therefore they create rituals around training; for most people, hygiene is a deeply held value, and therefore they create the ritual of brushing their teeth. If we hold our personal happiness as a value and want to become happier, then we need to form rituals around that, too.

What rituals would make you happier? What would you like to introduce to your life? It could be working out three times a week, meditating for fifteen minutes every morning, watching two movies a month, going on a date with your spouse on Tuesdays, pleasure reading for an hour every other day, and so on. Introduce no more than one or two rituals at a time, and make sure they become habits before you introduce new ones. As Tony Schwartz says, "Incremental change is better than ambitious failure. . . . Success feeds on itself."

Once you identify the rituals you want to adopt, enter them in your planner and begin to do them. New rituals may be difficult to initiate; but over time, usually within as little as thirty days, performing these rituals will become as natural as brushing your teeth.[3] Habits in general are difficult to get rid of—and that's a good thing when good habits are concerned. In Aristotle's words, "We are what we repeatedly do. Excellence, then, is not an act, but a habit."

People are sometimes resistant to the idea of introducing rituals because they believe that ritualistic behavior may detract from spontaneity or creativity—especially when it comes to interpersonal rituals such as a regular date with one's spouse, or artistic rituals such as painting. However, if we do not ritualize activities—whether working out in the gym, spending time with our family, or reading for pleasure—we often don't get to them, and rather than being spontaneous, we become reactive (to others' demands on our time and energy). In an overall structured, ritualized life, we certainly don't need to have each hour of the day accounted for and can thus leave time for spontaneous behavior; more importantly, we can integrate spontaneity into a ritual, as, for example, deciding spontaneously where we go on the ritualized date. The most creative individuals—whether artists, businesspeople, or parents—have rituals that they follow. Paradoxically, the routine frees them up to be creative and spontaneous.

Throughout the book, I will refer back to this exercise, as you introduce different practices, different rituals, that can help you become happier.

## Expressing Gratitude

In research done by Robert Emmons and Michael McCullough, those who kept a daily gratitude journal—writing down at least five things for which they were grateful—enjoyed higher levels of emotional and physical well-being.

Each night before going to sleep, write down at least five things that made or make you happy—things for which you are grateful. These can be little or big: from a meal that you enjoyed to a meaningful conversation you had with a friend, from a project at work to God.

If you do this exercise regularly, you will naturally repeat yourself, which is perfectly fine. The key is, despite the repetition, to keep the emotions fresh; imagine what each item means to you as you write it down, and experience the feeling associated with it. Doing this exercise regularly can help you to appreciate the positive in your life rather than take it for granted.

You can do this exercise on your own or with a loved one: a partner, child, parent, sibling, or close friend. Expressing gratitude together can contribute in a meaningful way to the relationship.

2

# Reconciling Present and Future

**Nature has given the opportunity of happiness to all, knew they but how to use it.**

—*Claudian*

One of the most important squash tournaments of the year was approaching. I had been training extremely hard and decided to supplement my training with a special diet. While my eating habits had always been quite healthful—a necessary part of my training regimen—I had occasionally allowed myself the "luxury" of junk food.

However, in the four weeks leading up to the tournament, I ate only the leanest fish and chicken, whole-grain carbohydrates, and fresh fruit and vegetables. The reward for my abstinence, I resolved, would be a two-day junk-food binge.

As soon as the tournament was over, I went straight to my favorite hamburger joint. I ordered four hamburgers, and as I walked away from the counter with my prize, I understood how Pavlov's dogs felt at the sound of the bell. I sat myself down and hurriedly unwrapped the first portion of my reward. But as I brought the burger closer to my mouth, I stopped.

For a whole month I had looked forward to this meal, and now, when it was right in front of me, presented to me on a plastic platter, I did not want it. I tried to figure out why, and it was then that I came up with the happiness model, otherwise known as the hamburger model.

I realized that in the month I had been eating well, my body felt cleansed and I was surging with energy. I knew that I would enjoy eating the four burgers but that afterward I would feel unpleasant and fatigued.

Staring at my untouched meal, I thought of four kinds of hamburgers, each representing a distinct archetype, with each archetype describing a distinct pattern of attitudes and behaviors.

## The Hamburger Model

The first archetypal hamburger is the one I had just turned down, the tasty junk-food burger. Eating this hamburger would yield *present benefit*, in that I would enjoy it, and *future detriment*, in that I would subsequently not feel well.

The experience of present benefit and future detriment defines the *hedonism* archetype. Hedonists live by the maxim "Seek pleasure and avoid pain"; they focus on enjoying the present while ignoring the potential negative consequences of their actions.

The second hamburger type that came to mind was a tasteless vegetarian burger made with only the most healthful ingredients, which would afford me *future benefit*, in that I would subsequently feel good and healthy, and *present detriment*, in that I would not enjoy eating it.

The corresponding archetype is that of the *rat race*. The rat racer, subordinating the present to the future, suffers now for the purpose of some anticipated gain.

The third hamburger type, the worst of all possible burgers, is both tasteless and unhealthful: eating it, I would experience *present detriment*, in that it tastes bad, and suffer *future detriment*, in that it is unhealthful.

The parallel to this burger is the *nihilism* archetype. This archetype describes the person who has lost the lust for life; someone who neither enjoys the moment nor has a sense of future purpose.

The three archetypes that I came up with did not exhaust all possibilities—there was one more to consider. What about a hamburger that would be as tasty as the one I had turned down and as healthy as the vegetarian burger? A burger that would constitute a complete experience with both present and future benefit?

This hamburger exemplifies the *happiness* archetype. Happy people live secure in the knowledge that the activities that bring them enjoyment in the present will also lead to a fulfilling future.

The graph on the next page illustrates the relationship between present and future benefit in the four archetypes. The vertical axis represents the future dimension of the experience, with *future benefit* on the top and *future detriment* on the bottom. The horizontal axis of the graph represents the present dimension of the experience, with *present benefit* on the right and *present detriment* on the left.

The archetypes, as I present them, are theoretical formulations of *types*, not of actual people. To varying degrees, and in different combinations, we all have characteristics of the rat racer, the hedonist, the nihilist, and the one who is happy. For the purpose of clarifying the essential characteristics, my descriptions will be like caricatures—resembling actual people, but with the distinguishing characteristics accentuated. To exemplify the archetypes we will follow the life of Timon, an imaginary character.

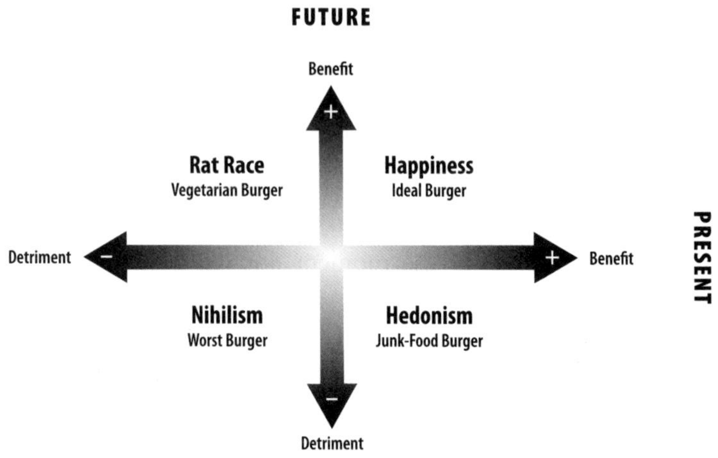


TIME-IN In which quadrant or two do you spend most of your time?

## The Rat-Race Archetype

As a young child, Timon is unconcerned with the future, experiencing the wonder and excitement of his day-to-day activities. When he turns six and goes to school, his career as a rat racer begins.

He is constantly reminded by his parents and teachers that the purpose of going to school is to get good grades so that he can secure his future. He is *not* told that he should be happy in school or that learning can be—and ought to be—fun.

Afraid of performing poorly on tests, fearful of missing a word of the teacher's gospel, Timon feels anxious and stressed. He looks forward to the end of each period and each day and is only sustained by the thought of the upcoming holiday, when he will no longer have to think about work and grades.

Timon accepts the values of the adults—that grades are the measure of success—and despite the fact that he dislikes school, he continues to work hard. When he does well, his parents and teachers compliment him, and his classmates—who also have been indoctrinated—envy him. By the time he enters high school, Timon has fully internalized the formula for success: sacrifice present enjoyment in order to be happy in the future. No pain, no gain. Although he does not enjoy his schoolwork or the extracurricular activities, he devotes himself fully to them. He is driven by the need to amass titles and honors, and when the pressure becomes overwhelming he tells himself that he will begin to have fun once he gets into college.

Timon applies to college and gets into the school of his choice. Joyful and relieved, he cries as he reads the acceptance letter. Now, he tells himself, he can finally be happy.

The relief, however, is short-lived. A couple of months go by, and Timon is again gripped by the same sense of anxiety he had been feeling for years. He fears that he will not be able to compete with the best students in the college. And if he can't compete with them, how will he get the job he wants?

His rat race continues. Through his four years of college, he works at building an impressive résumé: forming a student organization, becoming president of another, volunteering in a homeless shelter, and participating in varsity athletics. He chooses courses carefully—enrolling in them not because they excite him but because they will look good on his transcript.

Timon does have a good time every now and then, especially after handing in a paper or an exam. These pleasant moments, which come from being relieved of a burden, are short-lived; his work builds up again—and along with it, his anxiety.

In the spring of his senior year, Timon receives a job offer from a prestigious firm. He happily accepts it. Now, he thinks, he will finally be able to enjoy his life. Soon, however, he realizes that he does *not* enjoy his eighty-hour workweek. He tells himself that, once more, he must sacrifice for the time being, just until he is established and secure in his career. Once in a while, he feels good—when he receives a raise, a large bonus, or a promotion, or when people are impressed by his job title. The sense of fulfillment disappears, though, as drudgery returns.

After years and years of hard work and long hours, he is offered a partnership in the firm. He vaguely remembers thinking that he would be content if he became a partner—but he is not.

Timon was a top student in college; he is a partner in a prestigious firm; he and his wonderful family live in a large house in an upscale neighborhood; he drives a luxury car; he has more money than he can spend. Timon is unhappy.

Yet others regard him as the archetype of success. Parents see him as a role model, telling their children that if they work hard, they can be like Timon. He pities those children but cannot imagine what alternatives there are to the rat race. He does not even know what to tell his children: Not to work hard in school? Not to get into a good college? Not to get a good job? Is being successful synonymous with being miserable?

While Timon is an unhappy rat racer, it is important to note that there are many businesspeople who love to spend eighty hours each week immersed in their work. Being a hard worker, or a high achiever, is not synonymous with being a rat racer; there are supremely happy people who work long hours and dedicate themselves to their schoolwork or to their profession. What differentiates rat racers is their inability to enjoy what they are doing—and their persistent belief that once they reach a certain destination, they will be happy.

Moreover, in using Timon as an example, I am not suggesting that businesspeople alone are potential rat racers. A person pursuing a career in medicine may share the same attitudes and exhibit the same behavior: she feels pressured to get into a top medical school, then to find a good internship, then to become the head of the department, and so on. The same characteristic could apply to an artist who toils away at his art, unable to experience the joy he once derived from painting. His eyes are on the prize, on that "one big break" that will finally make him happy.

The reason why we see so many rat racers around is that our culture reinforces this belief. If we get an A at the end of the semester, we get a gift from our parents; if we meet certain quotas on the job, we get a bonus at the end of the year. We learn to focus on the next goal rather than on our present experience and chase the ever-elusive future our entire lives. We are not rewarded for enjoying the journey itself but for the successful *completion* of a journey. Society rewards results, not processes; arrivals, not journeys.

Once we arrive at our destination, once we attain our goal, we mistake the relief that we feel for happiness. The weightier the burden we carried on our journey, the more powerful and pleasant is our experience of relief. When we mistake these moments of relief for happiness, we reinforce the *illusion* that simply reaching goals will make us happy. While there certainly is value in relief—it is a pleasant experience and it is real—it should not be mistaken for happiness.

We can consider the experience of relief to be *negative happiness* as it stems from the negation of stress or anxiety. By its very nature, relief presupposes an unpleasant experience and cannot, therefore, yield lasting happiness. A person who is relieved of a splitting headache will feel happy that she is free of pain—but because that "happiness" had to be preceded by suffering, the absence of pain is but a momentary relief from an essentially negative experience.

The experience of relief is also temporary. When the throbbing in our head goes away, we derive a certain pleasure from the absence of pain but then very quickly adapt and take our physical contentment for granted.

The rat racer, confusing relief with happiness, continues to chase after his goals, as though simply attaining them will be enough to make him happy.

**TIME-IN** Do you, at times, feel part of the rat race? Looking at your life from the outside, what advice would you give yourself?

## The Hedonism Archetype

A hedonist seeks pleasure and avoids pain. She goes about satisfying her desires, giving little or no thought to future consequences. A fulfilling life, she believes, is reducible to a succession of pleasurable experiences. That something feels good in the moment is sufficient justification for doing it until the next desire replaces it. She initiates friendships and romances with enthusiasm, but when their novelty wears off, she quickly moves on to the next relationship. Because the hedonist focuses only on the present, she will do things that are potentially detrimental if they afford her immediate gratification. If drugs produce a pleasant experience, she takes them; if she finds work difficult, she avoids it.

The hedonist errs in equating effort with pain and pleasure with happiness. The gravity of this error is revealed in an old episode of "The Twilight Zone" in which a ruthless criminal, killed while running from the police, is greeted by an angel sent to grant his every wish. The man, fully aware of his life of crime, cannot believe that he is in heaven. He is initially baffled but then accepts his good fortune and begins to list his desires: he asks for an obscene sum of money and receives it; he asks for his favorite food and it is served to him; he asks for beautiful women and they appear. Life (after death), it seems, could not be better.

However, as time goes by, the pleasure he derives from continuous indulgence begins to diminish; the effortlessness of his existence becomes tiresome. He asks the angel for some work that will challenge him and is told that in this place he can get whatever he wants—except the chance to work for the things he receives.

Without any challenges, the criminal becomes increasingly frustrated. Finally, in utter desperation, he says to the angel that he wants to get out, to go to "the other place." The criminal, assuming that he is in heaven, wants to go to hell. The camera zooms in on the angel as his delicate face turns devious and threatening. With the ominous laughter of the devil, he says, "This *is* the other place."

This is the hell that the hedonist mistakes for heaven. Without a long-term purpose, devoid of challenge, life ceases to feel meaningful to us; we cannot find happiness if we exclusively seek pleasure and avoid pain. Yet the ever-present hedonist within each of us—longing for a Garden of Eden of sorts—equates effort with pain and doing nothing with pleasure.

In an experiment that illustrates a point similar to the one in the "Twilight Zone" episode, psychologists paid college students to do nothing: while their physical needs were met, they were forbidden to work. Within four to eight hours, students became unhappy, even though they earned significantly more money than they could have in other jobs. They needed stimulation and challenge and chose to leave their well-paying "cushy" job for work that was not only more demanding but also less financially rewarding.

In 1996 I conducted a leadership seminar for a group of South African executives who had been involved in the struggle against apartheid. They told me that, while fighting against apartheid, they had a clear sense of purpose, a clear future goal—life, though difficult and dangerous at times, was also challenging and exciting.

When apartheid was abolished, celebrations went on for months. As the euphoria waned, though, many people who had been involved in the struggle began to experience boredom, emptiness, even depression. Of course, they did not wish to return to apartheid—to the days when they were an oppressed majority—but in the absence of the cause to which they had dedicated themselves so fully, they felt a void. Some managed to find a sense of purpose in their family lives, in helping their community, in their work, or in their hobbies; others, years later, were still struggling to find a sense of direction.

Mihaly Csikszentmihalyi, whose work focuses on the state of peak performance and peak experience, claims that "the best moments usually occur when a person's body or mind is stretched to its limits in a voluntary effort to accomplish something difficult and worthwhile." A struggle-free, hedonistic existence is not a prescription for happiness. As John Gardner, former U.S. secretary of health, education, and welfare, points out, "We are designed for the climb, not for taking our ease, either in the valley or at the summit."

Let us now return to Timon, who, having failed to attain happiness by chasing one future goal after another, decides to focus on the present. He indulges in more drinking and drugs and engages in purely hedonistic relationships. He takes long breaks from work and spends hours sunbathing, enjoying the bliss of purposelessness, of not having to think about tomorrow. For a while, he believes that he is happy, but like the criminal in "The Twilight Zone," Timon quickly becomes bored and unhappy.

**TIME-IN** Think back to a time—a single experience or a longer period—when you lived as a hedonist. What were the costs and benefits of living this way?

## The Nihilism Archetype

In the context of this book, a nihilist is a person who has given up on happiness, who has become *resigned* to the belief that life has no meaning. If the rat-race archetype describes the state of living for the future and the hedonism archetype the state of living for the present, then the nihilism archetype captures the state of being chained to the past. People who have resigned themselves to their present unhappiness and expect the same sort of life in the future are fettered to their past failures to attain happiness.

Such attachment to past failures has been described by Martin Seligman as "learned helplessness." To study this phenomenon, Seligman placed dogs in three experimental groups. The dogs in the first group were given electric shocks, which they could turn off by pressing a panel. Dogs in the second group were given shocks that persisted regardless of their actions. The third group of dogs, the control group, received no shocks.

All the dogs were later put in boxes where they were given electric shocks but from which they could easily escape by jumping over a low barrier. The dogs in the first group (who had been able to stop the shocks earlier) and the dogs from the third group (who had not previously received any shocks) quickly jumped over the barrier and escaped. The dogs in the second group, who could not prevent the electric shocks earlier, made no effort to escape. They simply lay down in the box and whimpered while receiving shocks. These dogs had learned to be helpless.

In a similar experiment, Seligman subjected people to a loud and unpleasant noise. In one group, people were able to control the noise, to stop it, whereas people in the second group could not. Later, when both groups were subjected to loud noise that they could have turned off if they had tried, those in the second group did not try—they had resigned themselves to their predicament.

Seligman's work reveals how easily we can learn to be helpless. When we fail to attain a desired outcome, we often extrapolate from that experience the belief that we have no control over our lives or over certain parts of it. Such thinking leads to despair.

Timon, unhappy as a rat racer, equally unhappy as a hedonist, and aware of no other options, resigns himself to unhappiness and becomes a nihilist. What of his children, though? He does not want them to lead lives of "quiet desperation," but he has no idea how to guide them. Should he teach them to bear suffering in the present to attain their goals? How can he, when he knows the misery of the rat racer? Should he teach them to live simply for today? He cannot, because he knows too well the hollowness of the hedonistic life.

**TIME-IN** Think back to a time—a single experience or a longer period—when you felt nihilistic, unable to see beyond your current unhappiness. Had you been looking at the situation from the outside, what advice would you have given yourself?

The rat racer, the hedonist, and the nihilist are all, in their own ways, guilty of a fallacy—an inaccurate reading of reality, of the true nature of happiness and what it takes to lead a fulfilling life. The rat racer suffers from the "arrival fallacy"—the false belief that reaching a valued destination can sustain happiness. The hedonist suffers from the "floating moment fallacy"—the false belief that happiness can be sustained by an ongoing experience of momentary pleasures that are detached from a future purpose. Nihilism is also a fallacy, a misreading of reality—the false belief that no matter what one does, one cannot attain happiness. This last fallacy stems from the inability to see a synthesis between arrivals and floating moments, some third option that may provide a way out of one's unhappy predicament.

## The Happiness Archetype

One of my students at Harvard came to talk to me after receiving a job offer from a prestigious consulting firm. She told me that she was uninterested in the work she would be doing but felt she could not turn down this opportunity. She had had offers from many other companies, some for jobs that she would enjoy much more, but none that would "set her up" as well as this one. She asked me at what point in life—at what age—she could stop thinking about the future and start being happy.

I did not accept her question with its implicit either-or approach to happiness. I told her that instead of asking "Should I be happy now *or* in the future?" she should ask, "How can I be happy now *and* in the future?"

While present and future benefit may sometimes conflict—because some situations demand that we forgo one for the other—it is possible to enjoy both for much of the time. Students who truly love learning, for instance, derive present benefit from the pleasure they take in discovering new ideas *and* future benefit from the ways in which those ideas will prepare them for their careers. In romantic relationships, some couples enjoy their time together *and* help each other grow and develop. Those who work at something they love—be it in business, medicine, or art—can progress in their career while enjoying the journey.

To expect *constant* happiness, though, is to set ourselves up for failure and disappointment. Not everything that we do can provide us both present and future benefit. It is sometimes worthwhile to forgo present benefit for greater future gain, and in every life some mundane work is unavoidable. Studying for exams, saving for the future, or being an intern and working long hours is often unpleasant but can help us to attain long-term happiness. The key is to keep in mind, even as one forgoes some present gain for the sake of a larger future gain, that the objective is to spend as much time as possible engaged in activities that provide both present *and* future benefit.

Living as a hedonist every now and then has its benefits as well. As long as there are no long-term negative consequences (such as from the use of drugs), focusing solely on the present can rejuvenate us. In moderation, the relaxation, the mindlessness, and the fun that come from lying on the beach, eating a fast-food hamburger followed by a hot-fudge sundae, or watching television can make us happier.

**TIME-IN** Think back to a period or two in your life when you enjoyed both present and future benefit.

The rat racer's illusion is that reaching some future destination will bring him lasting happiness; he does not recognize the significance of the journey. The hedonist's illusion is that only the journey is important. The nihilist, having given up on both the destination and the journey, is disillusioned with life. The rat racer becomes a slave to the future; the hedonist, a slave to the moment; the nihilist, a slave to the past.

Attaining lasting happiness requires that we enjoy the *journey* on our way toward a *destination* we deem valuable. Happiness is not about making it to the peak of the mountain nor is it about climbing aimlessly around the mountain; *happiness is the experience of climbing toward the peak.*

## EXERCISES

### The Four Quadrants

Studies on journaling show that writing about negative as well as positive experiences enhances our levels of mental and physical health.[1]

On four consecutive days, spend at least fifteen minutes writing about your own experiences of the four quadrants. Write about a period of time in which you were a rat racer, a hedonist, and a nihilist. On the fourth day write about a happy period in your life. If you are moved to write more about a particular quadrant, do so, but do not write about more than one quadrant a day. Do not worry about grammar or spelling—just write. It is important that in your writing you describe the *emotions* you experienced then or are experiencing at the moment, the particular *behaviors* you engaged in (that is, what you did then), and the *thoughts* you had during the time or are currently having as you write.[2]

Here are some instructions for each of the quadrants:

- **RAT RACER:** Write about a period in your life when you felt as if you were running on a treadmill, living as a rat racer, for the future. Why were you doing what you were doing? What, if any, were some of the benefits to living that way? What, if any, price did you pay?

- **HEDONIST:** Describe a period in your life when you lived as a hedonist or engaged in hedonistic experiences. What, if any, were some of the benefits of living that way? What, if any, price did you pay?

- **NIHILIST:** Write about a particularly difficult experience during which you felt nihilistic, resigned, or about a longer period of time during which you felt helpless. Describe your deepest feelings and your deepest thoughts, ones you experienced then as well as ones that come up as you are writing.

- **HAPPY:** Describe an extremely happy period in your life or a particularly happy experience. In your imagination, transport yourself to that time, try to reexperience the emotions, and then write about them.

Whatever you write, as you are writing, is for your eyes only. If, after writing, you decide to share what you wrote with someone who is close to you, you can, of course, do so, but it is important that you not feel inhibited while doing the exercise. The more you open up, the more benefit you will derive.

Repeat the exercise at least two more times for the nihilism quadrant and for the happiness quadrant. When repeating the exercise, you can write about the same or different experiences. Revisit the entire exercise periodically—it could be once in three months, once a year, or once every two years.

## Meditating on Happiness

Research by the likes of Herbert Benson, Jon Kabat-Zinn, and Richard Davidson reveals the profound effects of regular meditation.

Meditate! Find a quiet spot. Sit down on a chair or the floor with your legs crossed. Make sure you are comfortable, with your back and neck straight. You can close your eyes or keep them open.

Enter a state of calm by breathing deeply through your nose or mouth, filling up the space of your stomach with each breath, and slowly releasing the air through your nose or mouth.

Mentally scan your body. If any particular part feels tense, direct your breath into that area to relax it. Then, for at least five minutes—or for as long as twenty—focus on your deep, slow breathing. If you lose your concentration and your mind wanders, simply and gently bring it back to your breathing.

Continuing with the deep breathing, focus on a positive emotion. You may imagine yourself when you were particularly happy, be it when you spent time with someone dear or when you thrived at work. For anywhere between thirty seconds and five minutes, reexperience the positive emotions and allow them to rise inside you. Especially after doing this exercise regularly, you may not need to imagine a particular event; you will have the capacity simply to bring up positive emotions by thinking of the words *happiness*, *calm*, or *joy*.

Make meditation a ritual. Set aside between ten minutes and an hour each day for meditation—in the morning when you wake up, during your lunch hour, or sometime in the afternoon. After meditating regularly, you may be able to enjoy some of the benefits of meditation in a minute or two. Whenever you feel stressed or upset or when you simply want to enjoy a moment of calm or joy, you can take a few deep breaths and experience a surge of positive emotions. Ideally, you should do this in a quiet spot, but you can also do it while riding the train, sitting in the backseat of a taxi, or at your desk.

3

# Happiness Explained

**Happiness is the meaning and the purpose of life, the whole aim and end of human existence.**

—*Aristotle*

We are all familiar with children's insatiable curiosity. Once they begin to question a certain phenomenon in the wonder-filled world around them, they do not relent. Why does it rain? Why does water rise to the sky? Why does water become gas? Why do the clouds not fall? Whether or not children get actual answers to their questions is of little relevance. Their relentless probing follows the pattern of the "infinitely regressive *why*"—regardless of the answer to a question, the child persists with another "Why?"

However, one question allows an adult to end the onslaught of "whys" without any feelings of guilt or inadequacy. This question is "Why do you want to be happy?" When questioning why we want certain things, other than happiness, we can always question their value with another "Why?" For example, why are you training so hard? Why do you want to win this prize? Why do you want to be rich and famous? Why do you want a fancy car, a promotion at work, a year off from work?

When the question is "Why do you want to be happy?" the answer is simple and definitive. We pursue happiness because it is in our nature to do so. When the answer to a question is "Because it will make me happy," nothing can challenge the validity and finality of the answer. Happiness is the highest on the hierarchy of goals, the end toward which all other ends lead.

The British philosopher David Hume argues that "the great end of all human industry is the attainment of happiness. For this were arts invented, sciences cultivated, laws ordained, and societies modeled." Wealth, fame, admiration, and all other goals are subordinate and secondary to happiness; whether our desires are material or social, they are *means* toward one end: happiness.

**TIME-IN** Do the "infinitely regressive *why*" exercise for a couple of things that you want—whether a bigger house, a promotion, or anything else. Notice how many "whys" it takes you to reach happiness.

For those not convinced by the argument that happiness should be pursued because it is the highest end, there is much research that suggests that happiness is also a means toward higher levels of overall success. In a review of the research on well-being, psychologists Sonja Lyubomirsky, Laura King, and Ed Diener note, "Numerous studies show that happy individuals are successful across multiple life domains, including marriage, friendship, income, work performance, and health." The research illustrates that the relationship between happiness and success is reciprocal: not only can success—be it at work or in love—contribute to happiness, but happiness also leads to more success.

All else being equal, happy people have better relationships, are more likely to thrive at work, and also live better and longer. Happiness is a worthwhile pursuit, whether as an end in itself or as a means toward other ends.

## Happiness Is . . .

Just when we believe that we have satisfied a child's curiosity, she will come up with another ploy. From the "infinitely regressive *why*," she will change course to the "infinitely regressive *what*" and the "infinitely regressive *how*." The questions "What is happiness?" and "How can we attain happiness?" require a more elaborate answer.

I define happiness as "the overall experience of pleasure and meaning."[1] A happy person enjoys positive emotions while perceiving her life as purposeful. The definition does not pertain to a single moment but to a generalized aggregate of one's experiences: a person can endure emotional pain at times and still be happy overall.

We may think about this definition in terms of the happiness archetype. Pleasure is about the experience of positive emotions in the here and now, about present benefit; meaning comes from having a sense of purpose, from the future benefit of our actions.

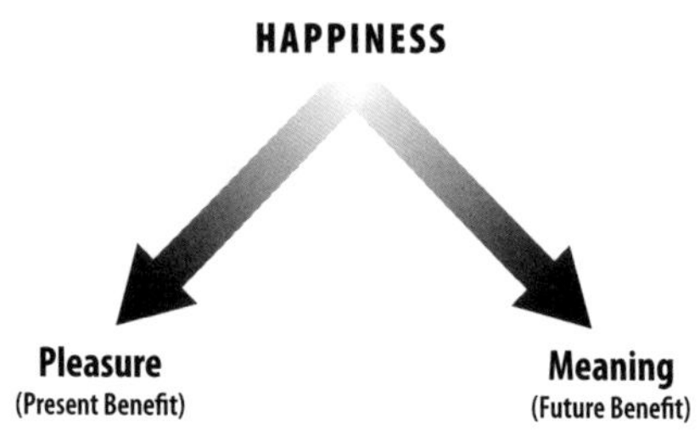


## Pleasure

Emotion, of course, plays a pivotal role in all our pursuits—including our pursuit of happiness. It is nearly impossible for us to imagine a life devoid of emotion. Think of an emotionless robot that, other than the capacity for emotions, has exactly the same physical and cognitive attributes as humans. The robot thinks and behaves in the same way that humans do. It can discuss deep philosophical issues and follow complex logic; it can dig ditches and build skyscrapers.

As sophisticated as the robot is, however, it lacks all motivation to act. This is because even the most basic drives are dependent on emotions—the one thing this robot lacks. The robot could not feel the satisfaction of eating or the need to eat; it could not experience the pain associated with hunger or the satisfaction of satiation. The robot would not pursue food and, given that it has the same physical needs of humans, would soon die.

But let us assume that the robot has been programmed to eat and drink regularly. Even then, despite continuing to live on the physical level, the robot would have neither motivation nor incentive to act. Attaining social standing, acquiring wealth, or falling in love would make no difference to it.

*Emotions* cause *motion*; they provide a *motive* that drives our action. The very language we use suggests an essential truth—that emotion, motion, and motivation are intimately linked. In Latin, *movere* (motion) means "to move," and the prefix *e-* means "away." The word *motive*, source of *motivation*, comes from *motivum*, which means "a moving cause." Emotions *move us away* from a desireless state, providing us motivation to act.

The neurologist Antonio Damasio provides an illuminating real-life example of the link between emotion and motivation. Following surgery for a brain tumor, one of Damasio's patients, Eliot, retained all of his cognitive abilities—his memory, mathematical ability, perceptual ability, and language skills. However, the part of Eliot's frontal lobe connected to the ability to experience emotions was damaged in the operation. Eliot's condition was similar to that of the emotionless robot: he had all the physical and cognitive characteristics of a normal human being, but the system "involved in feeling and emotion" was damaged.

Eliot's life changed dramatically. Prior to the surgery, he was a happily married, successful lawyer, but after the operation, despite the fact that his "rational brain" was not damaged, Eliot's behavior became so unbearable for those around him that his wife left him, he lost his job, and he was unable to hold another job for very long. The most striking thing about his predicament was his apathetic reaction: he no longer cared about his relationship or his career.

If we were devoid of emotion and hence of motivation to act, we would aspire to nothing. We would remain indifferent to our actions and thoughts, as well as their ramifications. Because emotion is the foundation of motivation, it naturally plays a central role in our motivation to pursue happiness.

However, merely being capable of emotion—any emotion—is not enough. To be happy, we need the experience of positive emotion; pleasure is a prerequisite for a fulfilling life. According to the psychologist Nathaniel Branden, "Pleasure for man is not a luxury, but a profound psychological need." The total absence of pleasure and the experience of constant emotional pain preclude the possibility of a happy life.

When I speak of pleasure, I am not referring to the experience of a constant "high" or ecstasy. We all experience emotional highs and lows. We can experience sadness at times—when we suffer loss or failure—and still lead a happy life. In fact, the unrealistic expectation of a constant high will inevitably lead to disappointment and feelings of inadequacy and hence to negative emotions. Happiness does not require a constant experience of ecstasy, nor does it require an unbroken chain of positive emotions.[2]

While the happy person experiences highs and lows, his overall state of being is positive. Most of the time he is propelled by positive emotions such as joy and affection rather than negative ones such as anger and guilt. Pleasure is the rule; pain, the exception. To be happy, we have to feel that, on the whole, whatever sorrows, trials, and tribulations we may encounter, we still experience the joy of being alive.

**TIME-IN** Make a mental list of things—from little things to big ones—that provide you with pleasure.

But is living an emotionally gratifying life really enough? Is experiencing positive emotions a sufficient condition for happiness? What of a psychotic who experiences euphoric delusions? What of those who consume ecstasy-inducing drugs or spend their days leisurely sprawled on the beach? Are these people happy? The answer is no. Experiencing positive emotions is necessary but not *sufficient* for happiness.

## Meaning

The philosopher Robert Nozick, in *Anarchy, State, and Utopia,* describes a thought experiment that can help us differentiate between the experience of a person on ecstasy-inducing drugs and an experience of true happiness. Nozick asks us to imagine a machine that could provide us with "the experience of writing a great poem or bringing about world peace or loving someone and being loved in return" or any other experience we might desire. The machine could afford us the emotional experience of being in love, which would feel the same as actually being in love. We would be unaware that we were plugged into the machine (that is, we would believe that we were actually spending time with our beloved). Nozick asks whether, given the opportunity, we would *choose* to plug into the machine for the rest of our lives. Another way of asking this question is, would we be *happy* if we were plugged into the machine for the rest of our lives?

The answer for most of us would clearly be no. We would not want to be hooked up to a machine permanently because we care about "things in addition to how our lives *feel* to us from the inside." Few of us would think that "only a person's experiences matter." We want not only to take pleasure in experiences, we "want them to be so." There is, then, more to happiness than positive emotions.

Circumventing the cause of these emotions, through a machine or drugs, would be tantamount to living a lie. Given the choice between a machine-generated feeling that we had brought about world peace and a less powerful feeling derived from actually helping one person, we would most likely choose the latter. It is as if we have an internal mechanism that demands more than the present sensation that we feel—we need the *cause* of our emotions to be meaningful. We want to know that our actions have an *actual* effect in the world, not just that we *feel* that they do.

As far as emotions are concerned, human beings are not far removed from animals, and some of the higher animals, like chimpanzees, have an emotional brain similar to ours. This is not surprising because without emotions (or sensations, in the case of some animals), there would be no drive to do anything, and a living organism would not sustain itself. Without emotions or sensations, animals, like the emotionless robot, would not move.

However, while our capacity for emotions is similar to that of other animals, we are fundamentally different. The fact that we can reflect on the cause of our emotions is one of the characteristics that distinguish us. We have the capacity to reflect on our feelings, thoughts, and actions; we have the capacity to be conscious of our consciousness and our experiences.

We also have the capacity for spirituality. The *Oxford English Dictionary* defines spirituality as "the real sense of significance of something." Animals cannot live a spiritual life; they cannot endow their actions with meaning beyond the pleasure or pain that those actions yield.

When speaking of a meaningful life, we often talk of having a sense of purpose, but what we sometimes fail to recognize is that finding this sense of purpose entails more than simply setting goals. Having goals or even reaching them does not guarantee that we are leading a purposeful existence. To experience a sense of purpose, the goals we set for ourselves need to be intrinsically meaningful.

We could set ourselves the goal of scoring top grades in college or owning a large house, yet still feel empty. To live a meaningful life, we must have a self-generated purpose that possesses personal significance rather than one that is dictated by society's standards and expectations. When we do experience this sense of purpose, we often feel as though we have found our calling. As George Bernard Shaw said, "This is the true joy in life, the being used for a *purpose* recognized by yourself as a mighty one."

Different people find meaning in different things. We may find our calling in starting up a business, working in a homeless shelter, raising children, practicing medicine, or making furniture. The important thing is that *we* choose our purpose in accordance with our own values and passions rather than conforming to others' expectations. An investment banker who finds meaning and pleasure in her work—who is in it for the right reasons—leads a more spiritual and fulfilling life than a monk who is in his field for the wrong reasons.

## Idealism and Realism

I once asked a friend what his calling in life was. He told me that he does not think about his life in terms of calling or some higher purpose. "I am not an idealist," he said, "but a realist."

The realist is considered the pragmatist, the person who has both feet firmly planted on the ground. The idealist is seen as the dreamer, the person who has her eyes toward the horizon and devotes her time to thinking about calling and purpose.

Yet when we set realism and idealism in opposition to one another—when we live as though having ideals and dreams were unrealistic and detached—we are allowing a false dichotomy to hold us back. Being an idealist *is* being a realist in the deepest sense—it is being true to our *real* nature. We are so constituted that we actually need our lives to have meaning. Without a higher purpose, a calling, an ideal, we cannot attain our full potential for happiness. While I am not advocating dreaming over doing (both are important), there is a significant truth that many realists—rat racers mostly—ignore: *to be idealistic is to be realistic.*

Being an idealist is about having a sense of purpose that encompasses our life as a whole; but for us to be happy, it is not enough to experience our life as meaningful on the general level of the big picture. We need to find meaning on the specific level of our daily existence as well. For example, in addition to having the general purpose of creating a happy family or dedicating our life to liberating the oppressed, we also need a specific purpose related to those goals, such as having lunch with our child or taking part in protest marches. It is often difficult to sustain ourselves with the thought of a general sense of purpose that lies far off on the horizon: we need a more specific and tangible sense that we are doing something meaningful next week, tomorrow, later today.

**TIME-IN** Think of the things that provide you with meaning. What can, or already does, provide a sense of purpose to your life as a whole? What daily or weekly activities provide you with meaning?

According to French Renaissance philosopher Michel de Montaigne, "The great and glorious masterpiece of man is to live with purpose." Having a purpose, a goal that provides a sense of direction, imbues our individual actions with meaning—and from experiencing life as a collection of disjointed pieces, we begin to experience it as a masterpiece. An overarching purpose can unify individual activities, just like the overarching theme of a symphony unifies the individual notes. In and of itself, a note does not amount to much, but it becomes significant—and beautiful—when part of a common theme, a common purpose.

## Potential and Happiness

When thinking about the most meaningful life for ourselves, we must also consider our potential and how to make full use of our capacities. While a cow might seem content with a life spent grazing in the pasture, we cannot be happy living simply to gratify our physical desires. Our inborn potential as humans dictates that we do more, that we utilize our full capacities. "The happiness that is genuinely satisfying," writes the philosopher Bertrand Russell, "is accompanied by the fullest exercise of our faculties and the fullest realization of the world in which we live."

This does not mean that a woman who has the potential to be the most influential person in her country cannot be happy unless she becomes president or prime minister, or that a person with the potential to be successful in business cannot be happy unless she makes millions. Becoming the president or a millionaire are *external* manifestations of potential. What I am referring to are *internal* measures of potential. The person with the capacity to be the president could be happy as a scholar of ancient Sanskrit; the person with the capacity to be a millionaire could lead a fulfilling life as a journalist. They can find satisfaction if they feel, *from within*, that they are doing things that challenge them, things that use them fully and well.[3]

**TIME-IN** What pursuits would challenge you and fulfill your potential?

## Success and Happiness

Some people might be concerned that pursuing meaning and pleasure over accolades and wealth could come at the price of success. If, for example, grades and getting into the best institutions no longer constitute a strong motivation, might not a student lose his commitment to his schoolwork? If promotions and raises are no longer the ultimate driving force in the workplace, will employees dedicate fewer hours to their jobs?

I had similar concerns about my own success as I was contemplating the shift toward the happiness archetype. The "no pain, no gain" formula had served me well, in terms of quantifiable success, and I feared that my resolve would weaken—that the next milestone would lose its appeal and no longer sustain me as it did when I was a rat racer. What happened, however, was the exact opposite.

The shift from being a rat racer to pursuing happiness is not about working less or with less fervor but about working as hard or harder at the right activities—those that are a source of both present and future benefit. Similarly, the shift from hedonism to the pursuit of happiness does not entail having less fun; the difference is that the fun the happy person experiences is sustainable, whereas the fun of the hedonist is ephemeral. The happy person defies the "no pain, no gain" formula: she enjoys the journey and, dedicating herself to a purpose in which she believes, attains a better outcome.

## The Need for Meaning and Pleasure

Just as pleasure is not sufficient for the attainment of happiness, neither is a sense of purpose. First, it is exceedingly difficult to sustain long-term action, regardless of the meaning we assign to it, without enjoying emotional gratification in the present. The prospect of a brighter future can usually keep us motivated for only a limited time. Second, even if we did sustain our denial of immediate gratification, as rat racers often do, we most certainly would not be happy.

In his book *Man's Search for Meaning*, Viktor Frankl talks about how victims of the Holocaust were able to find meaning in their lives. Despite the physical and emotional torture that these people endured in the concentration camps, some of them found meaning, a sense of purpose, in their meager existence. Their purpose could have been to reunite with loved ones or to someday write about what they had lived through. However, even to suggest that these people were happy while in the camp is absurd. In order to be happy, having meaning in life is not enough. We need the experience of meaning *and* the experience of positive emotions; we need present *and* future benefit.

My theory of happiness draws on the works of Freud as well as Frankl. Freud's pleasure principle says that we are fundamentally driven by the instinctual need for pleasure. Frankl argues that we are motivated by a will to meaning rather than by a will to pleasure—he says that "striving to find meaning in one's life is the primary motivational force in man." In the context of finding happiness, there is some truth in both Freud's and Frankl's theories. We need to gratify both the will for pleasure and the will for meaning if we are to lead a fulfilling, happy life.[4]

We, especially in the United States, are often criticized for being a society obsessed with happiness: self-help books offering quick-fix solutions and a struggle-free life are selling at an unprecedented rate, and there are psychiatrists who prescribe medication at the first sign of emotional discomfort. While the criticism is, to some extent, justified, it identifies the wrong obsession: the obsession is with pleasure, not with happiness.

The brave new world of quick fixes does not take into consideration long-term benefits and ignores our need for meaning. True happiness involves some emotional discomfort and difficult experiences, which some self-help books and psychiatric medication attempt to circumvent. Happiness presupposes our having to overcome obstacles. In the words of Frankl, "What man actually needs is not a tensionless state but rather the striving and struggling for some goal worthy of him. What he needs is not the discharge of tension at any cost, but the call of a potential meaning waiting to be fulfilled by him." As the science of psychiatry advances, it is likely that more and more people are going to be put on medication. While there are certainly many cases in which the use of psychiatric drugs is warranted and necessary, I am taking issue with the ease with which such medication is dispensed. There is a real danger that with the struggle, meaning too will be medicated away.

We should also remember that going through difficult times augments our capacity for pleasure: it keeps us from taking pleasure for granted, reminds us to be grateful for all the large and small pleasures in our lives. Being grateful in this way can *itself* be a source of real meaning and pleasure.

There is a synergistic relationship between pleasure and meaning, between present and future benefit. When we derive a sense of purpose from what we do, our experience of pleasure is intensified; and taking pleasure in an activity can make our experience of it all the more meaningful.[5]

**TIME-IN** Think back to a difficult or painful experience you had. What did you learn from it? In what ways did you grow?

## Quantity and Quality

We all enjoy and derive meaning from different activities, and to varying degrees. For example, writing provides me with both present and future benefit, but writing for more than three hours a day bores me. Watching two movies a week contributes to my happiness, whereas spending four hours a day in front of a screen, over time, will most likely frustrate me. Just because an activity provides us with meaning and pleasure does not mean that we can be happy doing it all the time.

To extend the food motif beyond the hamburger, I will introduce what I've come to call the *lasagna principle*—the notion that our capacity to enjoy different activities is limited and unique. Lasagna is my favorite food, and every time I visit my parents, my mother prepares a tray of it, which I promptly devour. This does not, however, mean that I want to eat lasagna all day and every day. The same principle applies to my favorite activities, such as writing and watching movies, as well as to my favorite people. Just because my family is the most meaningful thing in my life does not mean that spending eight hours a day with them is what would make me happiest; and not wanting to spend all my waking hours with them does not imply that I love them any less. I derive a great deal of pleasure and meaning from being with other people, but I also need my daily quota of solitude. Identifying the right activity, and then the right quantity for each activity, leads to the highest quality of life.

The best method of maximizing our levels of happiness is trial and error, paying attention to the quality of our inner experiences. Yet most of us do not take the time to ask ourselves the question of questions—because we are too busy. As Thoreau says, however, "Life is too short to be in a hurry." If we are always on the go, we are *reacting* to the exigencies of day-to-day life rather than allowing ourselves the space to *create* a happy life.

Abraham Maslow maintains that a person "cannot choose wisely for a life unless he dares to listen to himself, his own self, at each moment in life." It is important to put time aside to take Maslow's dare, to ask ourselves the type of questions that can help us choose wisely: Are the things that I am doing meaningful to me? Are they pleasurable? Is my mind telling me that I should be doing different things with my time? Is my heart telling me that I must change my life? We have to listen, really listen, to our hearts *and* minds—our emotions *and* our reason.

## EXERCISES

### Mapping Your Life

Though it is difficult to quantify internal states of mind and heart, it is still possible to evaluate our lives in terms of happiness and gain insight into how we can become happier. We could begin by recording our daily activities and evaluating them according to how pleasurable and meaningful they are.

Devoting a few minutes at the end of each day to write down and reflect upon how we spent our time can help us recognize important patterns. For example, we might realize that we spend a significant proportion of our time in activities that provide future benefit but that we do not enjoy, or doing things that provide us with neither meaning nor pleasure. We can then evaluate our lives through the lens of happiness and decide to add more meaningful and pleasurable experiences.

While there are basic principles that can guide us toward the good life—finding meaning and pleasure, for instance—there is no universal prescription for it. It is self-evident that human beings are complex, multifaceted, and different; each person is unique, a world unto himself. By zooming in on my day-to-day activities, I can see beyond the general principles that govern *a* life and identify the unique needs and wants of *my* life.

For a period of a week or two, record your daily activities. At the end of each day, write down how you spent your time, from half an hour e-mailing to two hours watching TV. This does not need to be a precise by-the-minute account of your day, but it should provide you with an overall sense of what your days look like.

At the end of the week, create a table listing each of your activities, the amount of time you devoted to each one, and how much meaning and pleasure each one provides (you can use a scale of 1 through 5, with 1 indicating no meaning or pleasure, and 5 signifying very high meaning or pleasure). Next to the amount of time, indicate whether you would like to spend more or less of your time on the activity. If you'd like to spend more time, write "+" next to it; if you'd like to spend a lot more time doing it, put down "+ +." If you'd like to spend less time on the activity, put "−" next to it; for a lot less time, write "− −." If you are satisfied with the amount of time you are spending on a particular activity, or if it is not possible to change the amount of time you devote to it at the moment, write "=" next to it.

Here is an example of part of such a weekly map:

| Activity | Meaning | Pleasure | Time/week |
|---|---|---|---|
| Spending time with family | 5 | 4 | 2.2 hours ++ |
| Meetings at work | 4 | 2 | 11 hours = |
| Watching TV | 2 | 3 | 8.5 hours − |

## Integrity Mirror

Make a list of the things that are most meaningful and pleasurable to you, that make you happiest. For example, a list could include family, exercising, promoting human rights around the world, listening to music, and so on.

Next to each of the items on your list, write down how much time per week or month you devote to it. With or without the help of the map you made in the preceding exercise, ask yourself whether you are living your highest values. Are you spending quality time with your partner and children? Are you exercising three times a week? Are you active in a human rights organization? Do you put time aside to listen to music at home and attend concerts?

This exercise raises a mirror to your life and helps you determine whether or not there is congruence—integrity—between your highest values and the way you live. With increased integrity comes increased happiness.[6] Given that we're often blind to the discrepancy between what we say is important to us and what we actually do, it may be useful to do this exercise with someone who knows you well and cares about you enough to be willing to help you evaluate your life honestly.[7]

How much time we choose to spend on our highest values depends on personal preferences and availability. Just because family is my highest value does not imply that to increase my integrity and therefore happiness I need to reallocate all the time I currently spend on my hobby to my family (remember the lasagna principle). A person who must work two jobs to get enough food on the table for his family is living in accordance with his highest values even though he gets to spend little time playing with his children.

Often, however, we are pulled away from the life that would make us happier by internal and external forces that we have some control over—such as our habits, our fears, or other people's expectations. Given that time is a finite and limited resource, we may need to give up some activities that are lower on our list of importance—say "no" to certain opportunities so that we can say "yes" to ones that are more valuable to us.

Repeat this exercise regularly. Change, especially of deeply ingrained habits and patterns, does not happen overnight. Most important, once again, is to ritualize your activities. In addition to creating a habit of activities that you want to engage in, introduce negative rituals—times during which you refrain from doing certain things. For example, if feasible, create an Internet-free time zone, each day between certain hours. We spend an increasing amount of time on the Web; checking our e-mail every few minutes takes away from our productivity and creativity and ultimately makes us less happy.[8] You can also introduce phone-free or meetings-free time zones, when you can fully focus on other activities, whether getting work done or spending time with your friends.

4

# The Ultimate Currency

**What lies behind us and what lies before us are tiny matters compared to what lies within us.**

—*Ralph Waldo Emerson*

Marva Collins was a schoolteacher in Chicago's inner city, a place where crime and drugs were rampant and where hope and optimism were scarce. The area's problems were grave, and many educators had little faith that their students would be able to escape the destitution and hopelessness that were passed down from one generation to the next.

In 1975 Collins founded the Westside Preparatory School for children in her neighborhood, many of whom had been rejected from other schools for bad behavior or for their inability, for one reason or another, to integrate into the school system. Westside Preparatory was their last chance before the street.

At Westside, these same children who were once labeled "unteachable" learned to read Shakespeare, Emerson, and Euripides by the fourth grade. The children who were once written off as irredeemable failures ended up going to college. Collins's students internalized her vision—that each and every student has the potential to succeed. They developed confidence in themselves and were able to imagine and realize a more hopeful future.

Collins founded her school with very little money, initially using her house as a classroom. For the next twenty years, she continued to struggle financially and was often on the verge of closure. Today, there are Marva Collins schools in several states; educators from all over the world come to Chicago to meet with her, learn her methods, and be inspired by her.

Collins's experience provides an insight into the implications of recognizing happiness as the ultimate end. She says that when "in the company of people who run multibillion [dollar] corporations and who have amassed fortunes," she asks herself time and again why she wants to be a teacher. Collins finds an answer as she reflects on one of her students:

> Tiffany was a child considered autistic and who had not spoken, who had been told by the experts that she was an unlovable and unteachable child. Then one day after much patience, prayers, love, and determination, Tiffany's first words to me were "I love you, Mrs. Ollins." The consonant *C* was left off; but I realized that the tears that flowed with Tiffany's declaration made me the wealthiest woman in the world. Today, to see Tiffany writing her numerals, beginning to read single words, talking, and most of all to see that glee in her eyes that says, "I, too, am special. I, too, can learn"—this to me is worth all of the gold in Fort Knox.

Of another student whose life was transformed by Westside Preparatory School, Collins writes, "It is worth all the sleepless nights wondering how I am going to balance our deficits to see the glow in [his] eyes that will one day light the world."

Marva Collins could have made a fortune. She could have avoided worrying about closures and deficits. In the 1980s she could have accepted the Reagan and Bush administrations' offers of the post of secretary of education and all the honor and prestige that that would have brought her, but Collins loved to teach and believed that she could make the most significant difference in the classroom.

Teaching gave her life meaning that she believed no other profession could give her; teaching gave her the emotional gratification that no amount of money could buy. She felt that she was "the wealthiest woman in the world" and that her experiences as a teacher were worth more to her than "all of the gold in Fort Knox" because *happiness, not gold or prestige, is the ultimate currency.*

**TIME-IN** What, for you, is worth all of the gold in Fort Knox?

## Happiness as the Ultimate Currency

If we wanted to assess the worth of a business, we would use money as our means of measurement. We would calculate the dollar value of its assets and liabilities, profits and losses. Anything that could not be translated into monetary terms would not increase or decrease the value of the company. In this case—in measuring a company's worth—money is the ultimate currency.

A human being, like a business, makes profits and suffers losses. For a human being, however, the ultimate currency is not money, nor is it any external measure, such as fame, fortune, or power. The ultimate currency for a human being is happiness.

Money and fame are subordinate to happiness and have no intrinsic value. The only reason money and fame may be desirable is that having them or the thought of having them could lead to positive emotions or meaning. In themselves, wealth and fame are worthless: there would be no reason to seek fame and fortune if they did not contribute, in some way, toward happiness. In the same sense that assets are secondary to money in a business—in that their worth is evaluated in dollars and cents—fame and material wealth are secondary to happiness in our lives.

The ramifications of understanding that happiness is the ultimate currency are dramatic. To take an extreme example, if we were offered the choice between a million dollars and a conversation with a friend, we should choose the one that would give us more overall happiness. If the conversation provided more emotional gratification and meaning than a million dollars, then we should choose the conversation. Using the ultimate currency as the standard, we would profit more if we were to choose the conversation.

Weighing the value of a conversation against money may seem like comparing apples to oranges. But by translating money, conversations, or anything else, for that matter, into the currency of happiness, through evaluating how happy something makes us, we have a common currency that enables us to compare seemingly unrelated experiences.

Needless to say, the choice between a million dollars and a conversation is not so simple. In order to choose wisely, it is insufficient to say that we enjoy speaking to our friend more and should therefore forgo the million dollars. A large sum of money can provide security in the future, and that may prevent certain negative emotions in the long run. In addition, a million dollars can provide the freedom and opportunity to take on meaningful tasks. If, however, after taking the full context into consideration, we find that the conversation will yield more pleasure and meaning, then it is ultimately of more value to us than a million dollars. As the psychologist Carl Jung said, "The least of things with a meaning is worth more in life than the greatest of things without it."

Imagine the following scenario. An alien from Venus walks into a shop and asks to purchase an item worth a thousand dollars. She offers the shop owner the choice between a thousand dollars or a bill that, on Venus, is equivalent to a million Earth dollars. The shop owner knows that he will never get to Venus and that Venusian money has no value on Earth. Unless he wants to keep the money for its sentimental value, the shop owner should choose the thousand Earth dollars. Venusian currency is only as valuable as the sum it can yield in the currency that is accepted on Earth.

Likewise, a million dollars is only as valuable as the sum it can yield in the ultimate currency. Just as Earth money is the ultimate currency in which a business is paid, and hence the currency that matters, happiness is the ultimate currency in which a human being is paid, and thus the currency that matters. Happiness should be the determinant of our actions, the goal toward which all other goals lead.

## Wealth and Happiness

Money—beyond the bare minimum necessary for food and shelter (and I am not talking caviar and castles)—is nothing more than a means to an end. Yet so often we confuse means with ends and sacrifice happiness (end) for money (means).

It is easy to do this when material wealth is elevated to the position of the ultimate end, as it so often is in our society. This is not to say that the accumulation and production of material wealth is in itself wrong. Material prosperity can help individuals, as well as society, attain higher levels of happiness. Financial security can liberate us from work we do not find meaningful and from having to worry about the next paycheck. Even so, it is not the money per se that is valuable but the fact that it can potentially yield more positive experiences. Material wealth in and of itself does not necessarily generate meaning or lead to emotional wealth.

Studies have shown that the relationship between wealth and happiness is very different from what most of us would expect. In extensive cross-cultural and longitudinal studies of happiness, psychologist David Myers found a very low correlation between material wealth and happiness, except in cases of extreme poverty where people's basic needs were not being met. Moreover, although for the last fifty years the population in many countries has become wealthier, studies reveal no increase, and often a decrease, in levels of happiness.

Nobel Prize winner in economics Daniel Kahneman has, over the last few years, turned his attention to studying happiness. Research by Kahneman and his colleagues found little support for the connection between wealth and positive emotions:

> The belief that high income is associated with good mood is widespread but mostly illusory. People with above-average income are relatively satisfied with their lives but are barely happier than others in moment-to-moment experience, tend to be more tense, and do not spend more time in particularly enjoyable activities. Moreover, the effect of income on life satisfaction seems to be transient. We argue that people exaggerate the contribution of income to happiness because they focus, in part, on conventional achievements when evaluating their life or the lives of others.

Surprisingly, some people feel more depressed once they have attained material prosperity than they did while striving for it. The rat racer is sustained by the hope that his actions will yield some future benefit, which makes his negative emotions more bearable. However, once he reaches his destination and realizes that material prosperity does not make him happy, there is nothing to sustain him. He is filled with a sense of despair and hopelessness, because there is nothing else to look forward to, nothing that will allow him to envision a future in which he would be happy.

There are countless examples of highly successful people who experienced depression and turned to alcohol and drugs. Paradoxically, "making it" actually made them less happy, for while they may have been unhappy before realizing their dream, they were often sustained by the belief that once they got there, they would be happy. And then they get there, and the "there" that they expected is nowhere to be found. Having been stripped of the illusion that most people live under—that material prosperity and status can provide lasting happiness—they are struck by the "what now?" syndrome. Realizing that all their efforts and sacrifices have not earned them the ultimate currency, they sink into learned helplessness. They experience nihilism and resign themselves to the fact that nothing could possibly make them happy, often turning to alternative means that are destructive in an attempt to escape their unhappy state.

So if material wealth does not lead to happiness, why the obsession with it? Why does being rich so often take precedence over finding meaning? Why do we feel so much more comfortable making decisions based on materialistic rather than emotional criteria?

Taking an evolutionary approach, it could be that our distant past determines our current behavior. When we were still hunters and gatherers, the accumulation of wealth—of food, primarily—

would often determine whether we would survive the next drought or the next cold winter. Hoarding became part of our constitution. Today, even those of us whose futures are materially secure still have the tendency to hoard far beyond our needs. The accumulation of wealth is no longer a means toward survival but an end in itself. We no longer accumulate to live; we live to accumulate.

In making decisions and judgments, we also tend to focus on the material rather than paying heed to the emotional because those things that are quantifiable lend themselves more easily to assessment and evaluation. We value the measurable (material wealth and prestige) over the unmeasurable (emotions and meaning).

In our material world, we worship material girls and boys. Wealthy people are revered by virtue of their material possession, as if net worth is an apt measure for how worthy a person is. Academics count number of publications as a key criteria for promotion. We measure the worth of a day or a week according to how productive we were and how much we got done. As Laurence G. Boldt says in *Zen and the Art of Making a Living*, "Society tells us the only thing that matters is matter—the only things that count are the things that can be counted." The monetary worth of a house is quantifiable; the feelings we attach to our home are not. Shakespeare's *Hamlet* may cost ten dollars in the bookstore; what it means to us cannot be measured.

**TIME-IN** Does concern over wealth and prestige detract from your overall experience of happiness? In what ways?

## Emotional Bankruptcy

While we are accumulating material wealth, we are nearing bankruptcy in the currency that truly matters. Just as a business can go bankrupt, so can a human being. To remain solvent, a business needs to make profits; that is, its income has to exceed its expenses.

In thinking about our lives, it may be helpful to think of positive experiences as income and negative ones as expenses. When our positive experiences outweigh our negative ones, we have made a profit in the ultimate currency. Long-term depression may be seen as a sort of emotional bankruptcy—the duration and intensity of negative experiences (losses) overwhelm the positive ones (income).

An entire society can face the prospect of bankruptcy—a great depression—if the percentage of individual bankruptcies continuously rises. Similarly, as the rates of anxiety and depression rise, society heads toward emotional bankruptcy in the ultimate currency. So while we are making huge strides forward in science and technology—in our material welfare—we are rapidly falling farther and farther behind emotionally.

Unfortunately, there are no signs that things are improving. Approximately one-third of American teenagers suffer from depression. Studies in the United States, Europe, Australia, and Asia indicate that children today experience more anxiety and depression than children did in previous generations. This trend extends across ethnic and socioeconomic lines.

In his book *Emotional Intelligence*, Daniel Goleman notes that "each successive generation worldwide since the opening of the [twentieth] century has lived with a higher risk than their parents of suffering a major depression—not just sadness, but a paralyzing listlessness, dejection, and self-pity, and an overwhelming hopelessness—over the course of life." What Goleman is pointing to here is the increase, society-wide, in the prevalence of emotional bankruptcy. The "overwhelming hopelessness"—the nihilism—that Goleman describes results from our sense that we are unable to overcome this impoverished emotional state, on either the individual or the global level.

According to Goleman, the "Age of Anxiety" that characterized the twentieth century is now evolving into an "Age of Melancholy." In *Man's Search for Meaning*, Viktor Frankl claimed that the "existential vacuum is a widespread phenomenon of the twentieth century" and lamented the fact that 25 percent of his European students and 60 percent of his American students felt that they lived in an "existential vacuum," a state of "inner emptiness, a void within themselves."

The situation today is worse than it was in 1950 when Frankl wrote his book, and a more recent survey of students entering American colleges may help to explain why. In 1968, college freshmen were asked what their personal goals were: 41 percent wanted to make a lot of money, and 83 percent wanted to develop a meaningful philosophy of life. The pattern was significantly different in 1997, when 75 percent of freshmen said their goal was to be very well off financially, and 41 percent wanted to develop a meaningful philosophy of life. As larger numbers of people come to perceive material wealth as an end in itself, and, thus, as more individual members of society are unhappy, society as a whole nears a state of emotional bankruptcy.

With emotional bankruptcy come some of our most disturbing social problems—including drug and alcohol abuse and religious fanaticism. It is easy to see why an unhappy person might take drugs if they provide him with a temporary escape from the reality of his joyless life or why someone might turn to a charismatic preacher who offers eternal happiness.

Happiness is not just a luxury, something to be pursued once all our personal and societal ills are resolved. Increasing the levels of the ultimate currency improves the quality of individual lives and can make the world a better, safer place.

# EXERCISES

## Sentence Completion

Sentence-completion technique was devised by the psychotherapist Nathaniel Branden, considered the father of the self-esteem movement.[1] This simple technique—generating a number of endings to an incomplete sentence—often helps people come up with insights that bring about meaningful change in their lives.

There are a few basic rules to this exercise. Quickly generate at least six endings—or as many as you can think of—to the sentence stem. You can do this in writing or speaking into a voice recorder. There are no right or wrong answers, and some of your answers may contradict each other. Put aside your critical mind; think after, not during. After you generate your responses, go over them and see whether you have learned anything important; it may take a few trials before you gain some insight.

If you do learn something new, act on it. While sentence completion works on the conscious as well as the subconscious levels, you will gain the most benefit if you consciously follow up on an insight.

Here is an example of a sentence stem completed with seven endings:

*If I bring 5 percent more awareness to my life . . .*
I will realize the price of saying yes too often.
I will no longer be able to avoid difficult situations.
I will appreciate my family more.
I will appreciate my life more.
Things could get more difficult.
I will spend more time with my family.
I will be kinder to my employees.

Following is a list of a few sentence stems taken directly or paraphrased from Branden's work:

If I bring 5 percent more awareness to my life . . .

The things that make me happy are . . .

To bring 5 percent more happiness to my life . . .

If I take more responsibility for fulfilling my wants . . .

If I bring 5 percent more integrity to my life . . .

If I were willing to say yes when I want to say yes and no when I want to say no . . .

If I breathe deeply and allow myself to experience what happiness feels like . . .

I am becoming aware . . .

Work on these sentence stems a number of times—you can do them every day for a couple of weeks or once a week for six months. You can do them all at once or do one or two at a time. If some sentence stems particularly resonate with you, repeat them for as long as you find them helpful.[2]

## Creating a Happiness Map

Look at the map you created as part of the exercise at the end of Chapter 3. Based on the data you collected, envision your ideal week. Once you have a picture, an image, of what you would want your life to look like, it is much more likely to become a reality.

If you want to spend more time with your family—say, eight hours a week—write it down. If you want to spend less time watching TV, write down the amount of time that you think is ideal—given all the other things you would like to do. Make it as realistic as you can; for example, even if ideally you would like to spend twenty hours each week reading novels and watching plays, it may not make sense given the other obligations in your life.

Are there things you do not do now that would yield high profits in the ultimate currency? Would going to the movies once a week contribute to your well-being? Would it make you happier to devote four hours a week to your hobby and to go out three times a week?

If you have many constraints and cannot introduce significant change, make the most of what you have. Consider what brief activities that provide you both future and present benefit you could introduce to your life. If a one-hour commute to work is uninspiring but unavoidable, try to introduce some meaning and pleasure to it. For example, listen to audiobooks or to your favorite music for part of the ride. Alternatively, take the train and use the time to read. Once again, ritualize whatever change you would like to introduce.

Periodically—once a year or so—repeat this exercise as well as the "Mapping Your Life" exercise from Chapter 3. Notice the progress you made and the areas where you would like to make further improvement as well as the ways in which your priorities may have changed since last year, thus necessitating some revision of the map.

5

# Setting Goals

**Happiness grows less from the passive experience of desirable circumstances than from involvement in valued activities and progress toward one's goals.**

—*David Myers and Ed Diener*

When, at age sixteen, I first embarked on my deliberate journey toward a happier life, I believed that to be truly happy, I would need to reach a desireless state—which to me meant to be free from wants and aspirations, without objectives and goals. After all, the goals I aspired to—like winning the championship—did not only fail to provide me with returns on my investment as far as the ultimate currency was concerned; they actually made me miserable, emotionally bankrupt. It took me a few years to understand that the problem was not with having goals—with having desires, wants, and aspirations—the problem was with the kind of goals I had, and the role they played in my life.

In fact, today I believe that goals are indispensable to a happy life—to be happy, we need to identify and pursue goals that are both pleasurable and meaningful. But before looking at the relationship between setting goals and feeling good, let's consider the relationship between setting goals and doing well.

## Goals and Success

People who set goals are more likely to succeed than people who do not. Having explicit objectives that are challenging and specific—with clear timeline and performance criteria—leads to better performance.[1] Setting a goal is about making a commitment in words, and words have the power to create a better future.

When it comes to the connection between goals and success, the science of psychology confirms, as it often does, what our language communicates, what some of the religious texts tell us, and what many people have experienced. The etymological connection between *concept* and *conceive* is not accidental. Through concepts, through words, we can conceive, give birth to, a new reality. In the Hebrew Bible, for example, God created the world with words: "Let there be light: and there was light." The book of John begins, "In the beginning was the word." The United States was declared into existence with a set of goals, objectives, and values.

Goals communicate, to ourselves and to others, the belief that we are capable of overcoming obstacles. Imagine your life as a journey. You are walking, knapsack on your back, making good progress, until suddenly you reach a brick wall that stands in the way of reaching your destination. What do you do? Do you turn around, avoid the challenge posed by the barrier? Or do you take the opposite approach and throw your knapsack over the wall, thus committing yourself to finding ways of getting through, around, or over the wall?

In 1879 Thomas Edison announced that he would publicly display the electric lightbulb by December 31, even though all his experiments had, to that point, failed. He threw his knapsack over the brick wall—the numerous challenges that he still faced—and on the last day of that year, there was light. In 1962, when John F. Kennedy declared to the world that the United States was going to land a man on the moon by the end of the decade, some of the metals necessary for the journey had not yet been invented, and the technology required for completing the journey was not available. But he threw his—and NASA's—knapsack over the brick wall. Though making a verbal commitment, no matter how bold and how inspiring, does not ensure that we reach our destination, it does enhance the likelihood of success.

William H. Murray, a Scottish mountaineer, wrote in *The Scottish Himalayan Expedition* about the benefits of throwing one's knapsack over a brick wall:

> Until one is committed, there is hesitancy, the chance to draw back; always ineffectiveness. Concerning all acts of initiative (and creation) there is one elementary truth, the ignorance of which kills countless ideas and splendid plans: that the moment one definitely commits oneself, then providence moves too. All sorts of things occur to help one that would not otherwise have occurred. A whole stream of events issues from the decision, raising in one's favor all manner of unforeseen incidents and meetings and material assistance which no man would have dreamed would come his way. I have learned a deep respect for one of Goethe's couplets: "Whatever you can do, or dream you can, begin it! Boldness has genius, magic, and power in it."

A goal, an explicit commitment, focuses our attention on the target and helps us to find ways of getting there. The goal can be as simple as buying a computer or as complex as climbing Mount Everest. Beliefs, psychologists tell us, are self-fulfilling prophecies, and when we commit, when we throw our knapsack over the brick wall, we demonstrate faith in ourselves, in our ability to achieve an envisioned future.[2] We create our reality rather than react to it.

**TIME-IN** Think of an experience or two where you committed to something. What were the consequences of your commitment? What are you committed to now?

## Goals and Well-Being

While empirical research and anecdotal evidence clearly show the connection between having goals and doing well, the relationship between goals and well-being is less straightforward. Conventional wisdom tells us that happiness is about the fulfillment of our goals. Decades of research, though, challenge our commonly held beliefs: while attaining a sought-after goal can provide much satisfaction, and the failure to attain a certain goal can lead to despair, these feelings tend to be short-lived.

Psychologist Philip Brickman and his colleagues demonstrated this by looking at the levels of happiness people had after winning the lottery. Within as short a period as a month, lottery winners return to their base levels of well-being—if they were unhappy before winning, they will remain so. Similarly, and perhaps even more surprisingly, accident victims who became paraplegic often are as happy as they were prior to the accident, within as little as a year after the accident.

Psychologist Daniel Gilbert extended these findings to show how poor most of us are at predicting our future emotional states. We think that a new house, a promotion, or a publication would make us happy, when in fact these achievements only lead to a temporary spike in our levels of well-being. The same applies to negative experiences. The emotional pain that comes with the end of a romantic relationship, losing our job, or the failure of our political candidate does not last long—we soon return to being as happy or as unhappy as we were prior to the experience.

The aforementioned research, in challenging some of our most strongly held beliefs about the role that goal attainment plays in our well-being, offers both good and bad news. The good news is that we can be less concerned about failure and therefore more daring in our pursuits. The bad news is that success doesn't seem to make much of a difference either—and if this is the case, it may seem like there is no point pursuing goals or, for that matter, pursuing happiness. Our life might seem then to resemble the life of Bill Murray's character in *Groundhog Day* or of Sisyphus eternally climbing the mountain.

Is the choice, then, either to be sustained by an illusion (that the attainment of certain goals will make us happier) or to face a brutal reality (that no matter what we do, we cannot become happier)? Fortunately not. There is another possibility, but it requires that we understand the proper relationship between goal and process, between destination and journey. When we understand this relationship, our goals can lead us to higher levels of well-being.

## The Role of Goals

Robert M. Pirsig, in *Zen and the Art of Motorcycle Maintenance*, describes joining a group of elderly Zen monks mountain-climbing in the Himalayas. Though Pirsig was the youngest member of the expedition, he was the only one who struggled; he eventually gave up, while the monks effortlessly ascended to the peak.

Pirsig, focused on the goal of reaching the peak of the mountain and overwhelmed by what still lay ahead, was unable to enjoy the climb; he lost his desire—and his strength—to carry on. The monks also focused on the peak, but only to make sure they were staying on course, not because reaching the peak itself was most important to them. Knowing that they were headed in the right direction allowed them to focus their attention and enjoy each step, rather than being overwhelmed by what still lay ahead.

The proper role of goals is to liberate us, so that we can enjoy the here and now. If we set off on a road trip without any identified destination, the trip itself is unlikely to be much fun. If we do not know where we are going or even where we want to go, every fork in the road becomes a site of ambivalence—neither turning left nor turning right seems a good choice as we do not know whether we want to end up where these roads lead. So instead of focusing on the landscape, the scenery, the flowers on the side of the road, we are consumed by hesitation and uncertainty. What will happen if I go this way? Where will I end up if I turn here? If we have a destination in mind, if we more or less know where we are going, we are free to focus our full attention on making the most of where we *are*.

The emphasis in my approach is not so much on *attaining* goals as it is on *having* them. In his article "Positive Affectivity," psychologist David Watson underscores the value of the journey: "Contemporary researchers emphasize that it is the process of striving after goals—rather than goal attainment per se—that is crucial for happiness and positive affectivity." The primary purpose of having a goal—a future purpose—is to enhance enjoyment of the present.

*Goals are means, not just ends.* For sustained happiness we need to change the expectations we have of our goals: rather than perceiving them as ends (expecting that their attainment will make us happy), we need to see them as means (recognizing that they can enhance the pleasure we take in the journey). When goals facilitate the enjoyment of our present experience, they indirectly lead to an increase in our levels of well-being each step of the way, as opposed to a temporary spike that comes with the attainment of a goal. A goal enables us to experience a sense of being while doing.[3]

While my argument is that having goals is necessary for sustained happiness, the mere existence of goals is not sufficient. The goals need to be meaningful and the journey they take us on needs to be pleasurable for them to bring about a significant increase in our happiness.

**TIME-IN** What goals have provided you with the most happiness in the past, in terms of facilitating a pleasurable as well as meaningful journey? What goals do you believe will do the same for you in the future?

Do all goals, as long as they provide meaning and pleasure, generate equal profits in the ultimate currency? What if, for example, making money is meaningful to me and prestige affords me pleasure? After all, the desire for material possessions and the need to be liked are part of human nature and, to varying degree, are important for most people. Given that, shouldn't the pursuit of wealth and accolades be an integral part of my pursuit of happiness?

Summarizing the research on goals and happiness, Kennon Sheldon and his colleagues write, "People seeking greater well-being would be well advised to focus on the pursuit of (a) goals involving growth, connection, and contribution rather than goals involving money, beauty, and popularity and (b) goals that are interesting and personally important to them rather than goals they feel forced or pressured to pursue." While most if not all people pursue popularity, beauty, and money—and, at times, feel forced or pressured to do something—Sheldon is pointing out that we would be happier if we shifted more of our focus to goals that are *self-concordant*. Research in this area provides us with a more nuanced understanding of the kind of meaning and pleasure that will maximize our potential for happiness.

## Self-Concordant Goals

Self-concordant goals are those we pursue out of deep personal conviction and/or a strong interest. These goals, according to Kennon Sheldon and Andrew Elliot, are "integrated with the self" emanating "directly from self-choice." Generally, for goals to be self-concordant, the person has to feel that she chose them rather than that they were imposed on her, that they stem from a desire to *express* part of herself rather than from the need to *impress* others. We pursue these goals not because others think we should or because we feel obligated to, but because we really want to—because we find them significant and enjoyable.

Research in this area indicates that there is a qualitative difference between the meaning we derive from extrinsic goods, such as social status and the state of our bank account, and the meaning we derive from intrinsic goods, such as personal growth and a sense of connection to others. Usually, financial goals are not self-concordant—they stem from an extrinsic rather than an intrinsic source. The desire for status and for impressing others is often, though not always, behind the pursuit of wealth.

In their research titled "The Dark Side of the American Dream," Tim Kasser and Richard Ryan demonstrate that pursuing financial success as a central goal in life, as a guiding principle, leads to negative consequences. Those for whom making money is the primary objective are less likely to actualize themselves and reach their full potential. They generally experience more distress and are more likely to be depressed and anxious. Moreover, given the mind-body connection, they are less healthy, less vital. The same results were found outside the United States: business school students in Singapore "who had strongly internalized materialistic values also reported lowered self-actualization, vitality, and happiness, as well as increased anxiety, physical symptomology, and unhappiness."

Psychologists doing research on self-concordant goals are not suggesting that we should cease from pursuing material possessions and accolades—to do so would be in a sense to wage war on our nature. Nor are they suggesting that the pursuit of financial security is unimportant. Having sufficient money to provide for food, shelter, education, and other basic needs is essential to our well-being. However, beyond providing these basic needs, money or prestige need not—and, if happiness is accepted as the ultimate currency, should not—be our central pursuits.

Money, though treated by most research on self-concordance as an extrinsic goal, can also function as an intrinsic objective—in which case wealth as a central pursuit would contribute to, rather than detract from, our happiness. Some people who strive to make more money care little about the material aspect of the wealth and much more about what it represents to them—reward for effort, a mark of competence, and so on. In this case, making money is associated with intrinsic factors, such as personal growth, rather than with extrinsic factors, such as social status.

Moreover, the pursuit of wealth can be translated into a self-concordant goal, if money is perceived and utilized as a means to meaning. For example, having money can free up our time to do things that are personally significant to us, or it can enable us to support a cause we believe in.

While there are clearly many benefits to identifying and pursuing self-concordant goals, it is anything but easy. Sheldon and Linda Houser-Marko note that selecting self-concordant goals "is a difficult skill, requiring both accurate self-perceptual abilities and the ability to resist social pressures that may sometimes push one in inappropriate directions." We first of all need to know what we want to do with our lives and then have the courage to be true to our wants.

**TIME-IN** What are some of your self-concordant goals? Are there any internal or external barriers that prevent you from pursuing these goals?

## Want-To Versus Have-To

The feeling that one has chosen one's goals freely is a precondition for self-concordance, which explains why people living in free countries are generally happier than those living under oppressive regimes. And yet many people in enlightened democracies spend much of their time feeling enslaved—not by the regime but by extrinsic factors that are self-imposed, such as prestige, a desire to please, obligation, or fear. They experience life as more or less a series of chores that they *have to* carry out rather than activities that they *want to* engage in. Have-tos, given that they are not self-concordant, usually lack meaning or do not afford pleasure—they are often devoid of both. Want-tos, being self-concordant goals, often provide us with both meaning and pleasure.

One way of becoming happier, increasing the base level of our well-being, is to reduce the have-tos while increasing the want-tos, in terms of general life pursuits as well as daily activities.

Do I pursue medicine primarily because I see it as meaningful (intrinsic factor), or is the social status associated with the profession my chief drive (extrinsic factor)? Do I choose trading first and foremost because of the excitement I derive from following the market (intrinsic factor) or because there is much money to be made (extrinsic factor)?

The preceding choices are not mutually exclusive. Most of our choices are driven by many factors, some intrinsic, others extrinsic. A person who goes into law to please his family surely also feels a sense of accomplishment when he helps bring about justice. Similarly, someone who becomes a lawyer because she is passionate about the law cannot remain indifferent to the status gained by success. The question is whether the intrinsic or extrinsic is more fundamental to the choice. If the primary driving force is intrinsic—in other words, the pursuit is self-concordant—then the person will experience it as something that he wants to do; if the primary driving force is extrinsic, the experience will be more of a have-to.

The same analysis that one applies to life pursuits can be applied to our daily pursuits. How much of my day is spent on activities that I want to do versus those that I have to do? Some have-tos are unavoidable. Personally I *want to* teach, but to do so I also *have to* spend many hours grading papers and exams. The challenge is not to entirely get rid of have-tos but to reduce them and, as much as possible, replace them with want-tos. How happy I am depends to a large degree on the ratio between want-tos and have-tos in my life. This ratio largely determines whether I look forward to getting up in the morning or am exhausted by the thought of what lies ahead; whether I feel a sense of accomplishment and satisfaction or more of a relief and release when the day, or the week, is over.

**TIME-IN** Think about a typical day. Do you have more have-tos or more want-tos? Generally, do you look forward to the start of the day or the week?

Asking ourselves what we want to do or what would provide us with both meaning and pleasure is often not enough. We need to dig deeper. My philosophy teacher, Ohad Kamin, gave me some advice when I graduated from college and was not sure where I wanted to go: "Life is short. In choosing a path make sure you first identify those things that you can do. Out of those, select the ones that you want to do. Then, reduce your choice further by zooming in on what you *really* want to do. Finally, select those things that you *really, really* want to do—and then do them." What Ohad did was to create four concentric circles for me, with the inner circle holding in it the pursuits that would make me happiest.

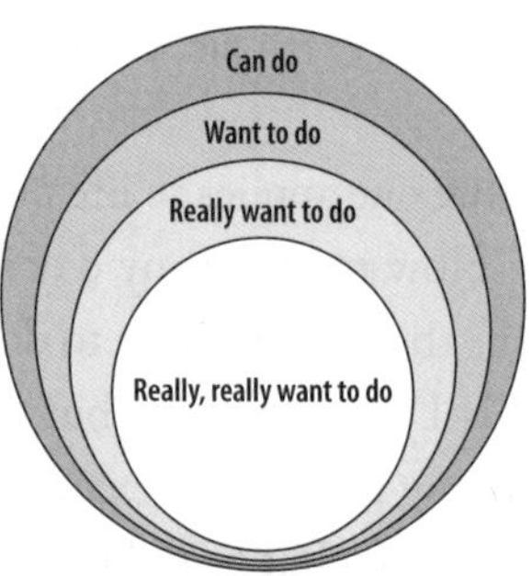


The outer circle captures the possibilities available to me. The innermost circle encompasses my deepest wants and desires. Pursuing these makes me feel most real and authentic—realizing my dreams as the author of my life. We do not always have the luxury to follow the prescription of the innermost circle—there are very often constraints that are outside of our control. However, genuine heartfelt and mindful answers to these questions can start us on a journey toward the fulfillment of our dreams. Words, after all, can create worlds.

**TIME-IN** What are the things that you really, really want to do?

My wife, Tami, and I often help each other set goals for ourselves—personal as well as joint ones. A few years ago, as I was talking about setting a *deadline* for one of the goals, she pointed out to me that because self-concordant goals inspire—literally, can put the spirit in us—it would be more appropriate to speak of *lifelines*. Similarly, when in pursuit of goals that are both pleasurable and meaningful, that yield both present and future benefit, we are *enlivening* time rather than *killing* time.[4]

According to Abraham Maslow, "Being focused on a task produces organization for efficiency both within the organism and in the environment." This is especially true when the task we focus on is self-concordant, aligned with our deepest interests and wants. In his final interview, twentieth-century scholar of mythology Joseph Campbell was asked by Bill Moyers whether he ever had the sense of "being helped by hidden hands":

> All the time. It is miraculous. I even have a superstition that has grown on me as a result of invisible hands coming all the time—namely, that if you do follow your bliss you put yourself on a kind of track that has been there all the while, waiting for you, and the life that you ought to be living is the one you are living. When you can see that, you begin to meet people who are in your field of bliss, and they open doors to you. I say, follow your bliss and don't be afraid, and doors will open where you didn't know they were going to be.

As research on self-concordant goals illustrates, Campbell's belief is much more than a superstition. When we follow our bliss, we not only enjoy the journey, we are also more successful. Devoid of a clear and personally compelling sense of direction, we are susceptible to aimless meandering and to being pulled away from our real, authentic self. When we know where we're going—and know that we really, really want to get there—it is much easier for us to stay on course, true to ourselves. We are more likely to say "no" to externally imposed obligations, to requests that are not aligned with our interests, to the sirens of status—and to say "yes" to the call, the voice coming from within.

Time is a zero-sum game, a limited resource. Life is too short to do only what we have to do; it is barely long enough to do what we want to do.

## EXERCISES

### Setting Self-Concordant Goals

People who articulate and pursue self-concordant goals are generally both happier and more successful. Write down what you really, really want to do for each of the key areas of your life—from relationships to work. For each, consider the following:[5]

- **Long-term goals.** These are concrete objectives, with clear lifelines, for anywhere between one and thirty years down the line. These should be challenging goals; they should stretch you. Remember that whether or not you actually achieve your goals is not the most important factor for long-term happiness; the primary objective of goals is to liberate you to enjoy the here and now, the journey. One of my long-term goals, for example, is to create a happiness curriculum that will include a series of books, lecture videos, and workshops by June 1, 2013 (in my goal-setting file, I elaborate on the actual books, the lectures, and the kind of workshops that I will create).

- **Short-term goals.** This stage is about dividing and conquering the long-term goals. What do you need to do, in the coming year, month, or day, in the service of your long-term goals? As I'm writing this now, one of my short-term goals, derived directly from my long-term goal, is to complete the first draft of this book by the end of this coming September.

- **Action plan.** What do you need to do, in the coming month, week, or day, in the service of both your short- and long-term goals? In your calendar, put down the actual activities that you need to carry out, either as a regular weekly or daily undertaking (these are your rituals) or as a one-time activity. What I'm doing at this very moment is part of my action plan: a daily ritual in which I put aside three hours to work on this book.

When we do not set explicit goals for ourselves, we are at the mercy of external forces—which rarely lead to self-concordant activities. The choice we face is between passively reacting to extrinsic demands and actively creating our life.

## Happiness Board

Create a personal happiness board—a group of people who care about you and your well-being, and who will hold you accountable to the ultimate currency. Ask your board members to keep track of your commitments and ensure that you follow through on them. Meet regularly to discuss your progress, where you have made significant improvements, where you would like to put more effort, or where you would like to change course.

Following up on our commitments and goals isn't easy. It takes time for a practice to become a habit, a ritual—and therefore most efforts at change ultimately fail. Change of any sort—be it starting an exercise regime, overcoming procrastination, or getting to spend more time with our family—is more likely to last when we enjoy the support of others.

In addition to creating your own happiness board, become a member of other people's boards (you may have one small group, in which you serve on one another's boards). By doing so, you will be helping them as well as yourself: by holding others accountable to the ultimate currency and reminding them to pursue meaningful and pleasurable activities, you will be indirectly strengthening your commitment to your own happiness.[6]

Part 2

# HAPPINESS Applied

6

# Happiness in Education

**Our best chance for happiness is education.**

—*Mark Van Doren*

My brother studied psychology at Harvard. Before he came to school, he spent his free time reading psychology, discussing it, writing and thinking about it. As a student, however, he disliked it.

His feeling was not unique: most students dislike schoolwork. What, then, motivates them to devote so much time to their studies? While talking to my brother about his unhappiness at school, I came up with two models that illustrate how students are motivated: the drowning model and the lovemaking model.

The drowning model shows two things: that the desire to free ourselves of pain can be a strong motivator and that, once freed, we can easily mistake our relief for happiness. A person whose head is forced under water will suffer discomfort and pain and will struggle to escape. If, at the last moment, his head is released, he will gasp for air and experience a sense of intoxicating relief.

The situation may be less dramatic for students who do not enjoy school, but the nature of their motivation—the need to avoid a negative consequence—is similar. Throughout the term, drowning in work that they do not enjoy, students are motivated by their fear of failure. At the end of the term, liberated from their books and papers and exams, they feel an overwhelming sense of relief—which, in the moment, can feel a lot like happiness.

This pattern of pain followed by relief is the model that is imprinted upon us from grade school. It is easy to see how, unaware of alternative models, living as a rat racer could seem like the most normal and attractive prospect.

The lovemaking model, however, offers a different way of thinking about learning, one that can encompass both present and future benefit. The many wonderful hours that we put into reading, researching, thinking, and writing can be looked upon as foreplay. The Eureka experience—when the boundary between knowledge and intuition breaks, when we reach a solution to a problem, for instance—is like the climax. As in the drowning model, there is a desirable end goal, but in the lovemaking model, we derive satisfaction from everything we do along the way.

Ensuring that the process of learning is itself enjoyable is, in part, the responsibility of each student, especially in college and graduate school, where they have more independence. Yet by the time students are mature enough to take responsibility for their education, most have already internalized the rat racer's ethos. They learn from their parents that grades and prizes are the measure of success, that their responsibility is to produce outstanding report cards rather than to enjoy learning for learning's sake. Educators—parents and teachers—who care about helping children lead happy lives must first themselves believe that happiness is the ultimate currency. Children are extremely sensitive to cues and will internalize their educators' beliefs even when these beliefs are implicit.

In school, children should be encouraged to pursue the paths that afford them pleasure and meaning. If a student wants to be a social worker and has taken the time to consider the costs and benefits of such a career, then his teachers should encourage him even though he might earn more as an investment banker. If he wants to become a businessman, then his parents should support him, even though their wish had always been that he pursue politics. For parents and teachers who believe that happiness is the ultimate currency, this is the natural and logical thing to do.[1]

**TIME-IN** Think of the best teacher you had in school. What did he or she do to draw the love of learning out of you?

In emphasizing achievements (which are tangible) over the cultivation of a love of learning (which is intangible), schools simultaneously reinforce the rat-race mentality and stifle children's emotional development. The rat racer learns that emotional gratification is secondary to the kind of achievements that others can recognize and validate, that emotions only get in the way of success and are best ignored or suppressed.

The irony is that emotions are necessary not only for the pursuit of the ultimate currency but for the attainment of material success as well. Daniel Goleman, in *Emotional Intelligence*, says, "Psychologists agree that IQ contributes only about 20 percent of the factors that determine success. A full 80 percent comes from other factors, including what I call emotional intelligence." The mind-set of the rat racer is antithetical to emotional intelligence and thus to a happy *and* successful life.

What, then, can teachers and parents do to help students experience pleasure in school and at the same time perform well? How can achievement and the love of learning be reconciled? The work of psychologist Mihaly Csikszentmihalyi on "flow" provides us with important insights and guidelines on how we can create environments at home and school that are conducive to the experience of present and future benefit, pleasure and meaning.

## Flow

Flow, according to Csikszentmihalyi, is a state in which one is immersed in an experience that is rewarding in and of itself, a state in which we feel we are one with the experience, in which "action and awareness are merged."[2]

We all know what it feels like to be so absorbed in reading a book or writing a paper that we fail to hear our name being called. Or while cooking a meal or talking to a friend or playing basketball in the neighborhood park, we discover that hours have gone by when it seemed that only minutes had passed. These are experiences of flow.

When in a state of flow we enjoy both peak experience *and* peak performance: we experience pleasure and perform at our best. Athletes often refer to this experience as being in the zone. Whatever we do in a state of flow—whether kicking a ball, carving wood, writing a poem, or studying for an exam—we are completely focused on our activity; nothing distracts us or competes for our attention. Performing at our best, we learn, grow, improve, and advance toward our future purpose.

Csikszentmihalyi explains that having goals, having a clear sense of purpose, is necessary in order to attain flow. While goals can and do change over time, the direction of the activity has to be unambiguous while we are performing it. When we are not distracted by all the other possible things we could be doing, when we are wholeheartedly committed to our objective, we are free to devote ourselves fully to the task at hand. As I discussed earlier in the chapter on goals, having a clear destination in mind liberates us to enjoy the journey. In flow, present and future benefit merge: a clear future goal is not in opposition but rather contributes to the experience of the here and now. Flow experiences lead to higher levels of happiness by transforming the formula of "no pain, no gain" to "present gain, future gain."

Csikszentmihalyi's studies of flow show that the "no pain, no gain" model is based on the myth that only through extreme and sustained overexertion can we attain our optimal level of performance. Research on flow shows that pain is not, in fact, the optimal condition for peak performance. Rather, there is a specific zone, the line between overexertion and underexertion, where we not only perform at our best but also enjoy what we are doing. We reach this zone when our activities provide the appropriate level of challenge, when the task at hand is neither too difficult nor too easy.

The graph shows that if the difficulty of a task is high and our skill level is low, then we experience anxiety; if our skill level is high and the difficulty of the task is low, we experience boredom.

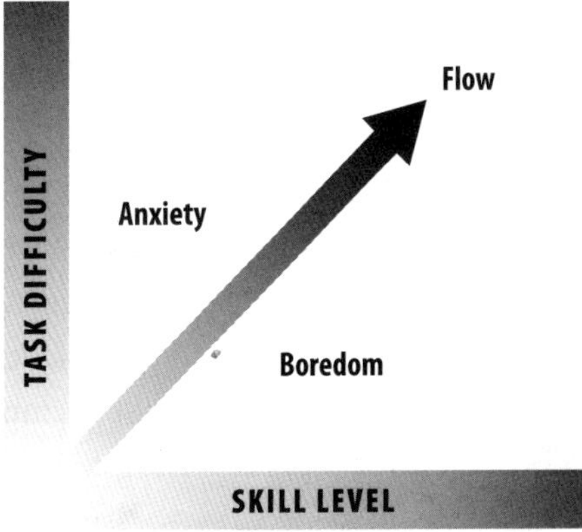

We experience flow when the difficulty of the task and our skill level correspond.

**TIME-IN** When do you experience flow?

Because many students experience either boredom or anxiety in school, they neither enjoy it nor perform at their best. For students to derive more present and future benefit from school, teachers should, whenever possible, structure lessons and activities to meet the skill level of each individual student. As the graph suggests, there are two distinct ways of hurting students' prospects of experiencing flow. First, by creating a stressful environment, leading to anxiety; second, by creating an environment that is devoid of struggle and challenge, leading to boredom.

In the first case, the teacher applies the drowning model to the child's education. The child is pushed too hard, beyond her stretch zone, and schoolwork becomes synonymous with pain, anxiety, and unhappiness. She is encouraged to focus on outcome rather than process, on the destination rather than the journey. The child very quickly becomes a rat racer, finding it hard to experience flow not only in school but also throughout her life—at work and in leisure.

In the second case, rather than overexertion and anxiety, there is underexertion and boredom. The consequences of too little struggle are no less detrimental than too much struggle, and they go beyond flow deprivation. Educators, especially parents, confuse struggle with pain; wanting to protect their children from pain, they cater to their children's every wish and rescue them from every challenge. In trying to provide a "privileged" life for their children, these parents deny them the opportunity to struggle, thereby keeping them from experiencing flow as well as the satisfaction of overcoming challenges.

When I was growing up, my favorite cartoon was *Richie Rich: The Poor Little Rich Boy*, about the struggles of a child who, seemingly, had it all. The oxymoron in the title, of being poor and rich simultaneously, makes perfect sense if we invoke the ultimate currency: in our relatively well-to-do society, we see an increasing number of wealthy children—and adults—who are unhappy. Some refer to this phenomenon as a form of "affluenza"; I have come to think of it as the underprivilege of privilege.

## The Underprivilege of Privilege

Samuel Smiles, father of the modern self-help movement, wrote in 1858 that "every youth should be made to feel that his happiness and well-doing in life must necessarily rely mainly on himself and the exercise of his own energies, rather than upon the help and patronage of others." When parents "help" their children circumvent hard work, it can lead to much unhappiness in the long run: "It is doubtful whether any heavier curse could be imposed on man than the complete gratification of all his wishes without effort on his part, leaving nothing for his hopes, desires, or struggles." When challenged, children, like adults, will find meaning in their accomplishments and enjoy the process of attaining their goals.

The underprivilege of privilege can explain, to some extent, why in this culture of relative plenty levels of depression are on the rise and why depression is hitting at a younger age than ever before. Life, for many young people, has quite literally been too easy.

Struggles and hardships and challenges are a necessary component of an emotionally rich life; there are no easy shortcuts to happiness. And yet our immediate response to others' struggles—especially if those others happen to be our children—is to want to make things easier. Letting them struggle when we have the means to make life easier seems unnatural; but there are times when we have to curb our impulse and allow them the privilege of hardship.

Unhappiness is also common among the rich because they are under increased pressure to feel happy. I've encountered this phenomenon among a number of my students who come from a privileged background. "What possible right or reason," a student would often ask, "do I have to be unhappy?" He feels guilty for being ungrateful, for not fully appreciating his lot in life. Moreover, because he cannot find a good reason for being unhappy, he blames himself for his predicament and feels inadequate. The pressure to be happy—the feelings of guilt and inadequacy in the face of negative emotions—leads to further unhappiness. What he and many others in our material world fail to recognize is that emotions are largely indifferent to material wealth.

## Emotions as the Great Equalizer

We all have the capacity for, and we all experience, great pain, great joy, and everything in between. While not all people have the same access to material goods, most have equal access to the ultimate currency. As I pointed out earlier in the book, aside from those who are living under conditions of extreme poverty or political oppression, happiness and unhappiness are equally distributed in the population. In their article "Who Is Happy?" David Myers and Ed Diener summarize research on subjective well-being: "Happiness and life satisfaction are similarly available to the young and the old, women and men, blacks and whites, the rich and the working-class." The ultimate currency is the great equalizer.

In the words of eighteenth-century economist and philosopher Adam Smith, "In what constitutes the real happiness of human life, they [the poorer class] are in no respect inferior to those who would seem so much above them." While Smith wrote from the vantage point of the privileged class—and with an aloofness characteristic of his time—he is right that we have no reason to believe that the pain or joy of the poor is different in quality or quantity from that of the rich. Once basic needs—food, shelter, and adequate education—are met, not much distinguishes among different income groups in the realm of emotions.

The unhappiness of the rich is no less real, no less natural, no less prevalent than the unhappiness of the poor, and it is therefore no less justified. We all, at different times throughout our lives, experience sadness and anxiety and joy and happiness; depriving ourselves of the permission to experience any or all of these emotions makes us underprivileged in the ultimate currency, whether or not we are materially well-off. No privilege in the world can protect us from experiencing emotional pain, even nihilism at times, and the expectations that it should only leads to further unhappiness. We, regardless of our income and social status, need to give ourselves the permission to be human.[3]

**TIME-IN** Do you accept negative emotions as natural or do you reject them? Do you give yourself the permission to be human?

## Prejudice Against Work

Csikszentmihalyi's research shows that twelve-year-old children already make a clear distinction between work and play, a distinction that stays with most of us for the rest of our lives. It is very clear to children that their education is about schoolwork, homework, and hard work. Perceiving school as work largely prevents students from enjoying their educational experience, because there is a society-wide prejudice against work. This prejudice is deeply rooted in the Western psyche and can be traced to our most influential texts.

Adam and Eve lived the quintessential life of leisure—they did not work and did not plan for the future. Yet when they ate the forbidden fruit, they were banished from the Garden of Eden, and they and their descendants were condemned to lives of hard work. The notion of hard work as punishment has become so embedded in our culture that we tend to depict heaven—the ideal place in which we would have the ideal life—as devoid of every hardship, including work. As it turns out, though, here on earth we do need to work to be happy.

In their article "Optimal Experience in Work and Leisure," Csikszentmihalyi and Judith LeFevre show that people prefer leisure to work, a conclusion that no one would find startling. However, they also discovered something else: that people actually have more flow experiences at work than they do at home.

This paradox—that we say we prefer leisure at the same time that we are having our peak experiences at work—is strange and revealing. It suggests that our prejudice against work, our association of effort with pain and leisure with pleasure, is so deep-rooted that it distorts our perception of the actual experience. When we automatically and regularly evaluate positive experiences at work negatively, simply as a learned response, we are severely limiting our potential for happiness—because in order to be happy we must not only experience positive emotions but also evaluate them as such.

Work can, and ought to, be a place in which we experience positive emotions. In *The Courage to Teach*, educator Parker Palmer writes that "in a culture that sometimes equates work with suffering, it is revolutionary to suggest that the best inward sign of vocation is deep gladness—revolutionary but true." Our equating work and effort with pain and suffering poses an internal barrier that prevents many people from experiencing happiness at school and in the workplace.

To help us experience more joy in school and in the workplace, we can cognitively reframe our experience—rid ourselves of the prejudice we have against work. A study run by Donald Hebb back in 1930 can help us understand how this reframing can take place.

Six hundred students between the ages of six and fifteen were told that they no longer needed to do any schoolwork. If they misbehaved in class, their punishment was to go out and play; if they behaved, their reward was getting to do more work. Hebb reports, "In these circumstances, all of the pupils discovered within a day or two that, within limits, they preferred work to no work (and incidentally learned more arithmetic and so forth than in previous years)." If we can learn to reframe our work and our education as a *privilege* rather than as a *duty*—and do the same for our children—we will be much better off in the ultimate currency. Not only that, but we will also learn more and perform better.

**TIME-IN** Can you learn to see your experience of school or work as a privilege? What do you, or can you, enjoy in this experience?

When our vision of happiness is rigid—when it precludes the possibility that effort and struggle can be sources of the ultimate currency—we overlook some of the best prospects we have to create a fulfilling life. In school or at work, we fail to recognize and realize opportunities for happiness; outside of school and work, we squander our "free" time by freeing it of effort, of challenge, and, hence, of much meaning. We are then left with a feeling that happiness is hopelessly elusive.

Education, at its best, ought to help students prosper materially and emotionally. To do so, schools must focus on more than the technical aspects of education—they must go beyond the three *R*s (w*R*iting, *R*eading, and a*R*ithmetic). I suggest a fourth *R*: *R*evelry. Teachers need to create the conditions in school that will allow students to revel in learning, in growing, in life itself. Most of us spend many years in the classroom, and many of our expectations and habits are established during these formative years. If, in school, students are encouraged to pursue happiness, to focus on activities that will generate the ultimate currency, they are more likely to do the same throughout their lives; if, on the other hand, all they do is race like rats, from one grade to the next, they are more likely to continue along this path long after graduation day.

Rather than helping students find meaningful and challenging goals and activities, rather than helping students experience the joy of learning, many educators are more concerned with getting students to score well on exams. Csikszentmihalyi writes:

> Neither parents nor schools are very effective at teaching the young to find pleasure in the right things. Adults, themselves often deluded by infatuation with fatuous models, conspire in the deception. They make serious tasks seem dull and hard, and frivolous ones exciting and easy. Schools generally fail to teach how exciting, how mesmerizingly beautiful science or mathematics can be; they teach the routine of literature or history rather than the adventure.

The love of learning is hardwired: young children are always asking questions, are always eager to find out more about the world around them. Educators who support children in the pursuit of the things that are important to them and who help children attain flow experiences cultivate this innate love of learning. They can turn education into a mesmerizingly beautiful adventure—the lifelong pursuit of the ultimate currency.

## EXERCISES

### Education Program

The most successful people are lifelong learners; they constantly ask questions and never cease to explore the wonder-filled world around them. Regardless of where you are in life—whether you are fifteen or a hundred and fifteen, whether you are going through a rough patch or are thriving—create an education program for yourself.

Your program can include the following two categories: personal development and professional development. Under each category, commit to learning material that will yield both present benefit (that you enjoy reading and thinking about) as well as future benefit (that will contribute to your overall growth). Ritualize your program by putting aside regular times each week for your education.

For example, under the personal development category, commit to reading Nathaniel Branden's *The Six Pillars of Self-Esteem* and doing the sentence-completion program in it. In addition, pledge to take a positive psychology course at your local college and to keep a personal journal. For professional development, you may wish to seek out a mentor whom you trust, as well as read up on the latest developments in your industry.

### The Privilege of Hardship

While I do not believe that things necessarily happen for the best, I know that some people are able to make the best of things that happen. Hardship, which we would never voluntarily invite into our life, can play an important role in our development; a struggle-free life is not always the best thing for us.

Write about a difficult experience that you went through—a particular failure or a longer period during which you struggled. After describing it in as much detail as possible, write about some of the lessons and benefits that came about as a result of the experience. Without minimizing or trivializing the pain associated with the experience, write down what profits, especially in the ultimate currency, you were able to eventually derive. Did it make you more resilient? Did you learn important lessons? Are you more appreciative of certain things now? Are there other lessons that you can learn from it?

If you do this exercise in a group, help one another identify more benefits that can be derived from the experience. Make the most of the difficulty. As my colleague Anne Harbison once said, "Never let a good crisis go to waste."

7

# Happiness in the Workplace

**Taste the joy that springs from labor.**

*—Henry Wadsworth Longfellow*

Ten years ago I met a young man, a corporate lawyer, who was working in a prestigious New York firm and was about to be made partner. He owned a luxury apartment overlooking Central Park and had just bought a new BMW, for cash.

He worked extremely hard, spending at least sixty hours each week in the office. Every morning he had to drag himself out of bed to get there, for he felt that he had very little to which he could look forward—the meetings with clients and colleagues and the legal briefs and contracts that filled his days were nothing more to him than a series of chores to be gotten through.

When I asked him what he would do for a living in an ideal world, he said that he would work in an art gallery. Were no jobs available in art galleries? No, no, he told me, there were jobs. Was he not qualified to find work? He was. But working in an art gallery, he said, would entail a steep loss of income and lowered standard of living. He hated the law firm but saw no way out.

Here was a man who was unhappy because he felt enslaved to a job he disliked. And he's not alone in his unhappiness; in the United States, only 50 percent of employees say that they are satisfied with their work.[1] Yet my conversation with the lawyer, and with many others who were dissatisfied at work, made clear to me that they were enslaved not because they had no choice but because they had made a choice that made them unhappy.

## Slave to Passions

In Hebrew, the word for "work" (*avoda*) stems from the same root as the word for "slave" (*eved*). Most of us have no choice but to work for a living. Even if we do not need to work for our survival, we are enslaved by our nature: we are constituted to want to be happy, and to be happy we need to work.

However, being enslaved by the exigencies of life and by our constitution does not preclude the possibility that we can *feel* free. We experience freedom when we *choose* a path that provides us both meaning and pleasure. Whether or not our subjective experience of work is of freedom depends on whether we choose to be slaves to material wealth or to emotional prosperity, slaves to others' expectations or to our passions.

To make such choices, we might begin by asking some questions of ourselves. Ask and you shall receive, say the Scriptures. When we ask questions, we open ourselves up to new quests and conquests: we see things we may not have seen before, discover paths that were previously obscured.

By posing a series of genuine questions, we challenge our assumptions, our conventional ways of thinking about what is possible in our lives: Am I happy at work? How can I become happier? Can I leave my job and find something meaningful and pleasurable? If I cannot afford to leave or, for one reason or another, do not want to leave, what can I do to make my work more enjoyable?

The right employer can create conditions that are conducive to happiness. For example, research conducted by psychologist Richard Hackman illustrates that certain conditions can lead an employee to experience more meaning in her work. First, the work should draw out a variety of talents and skills; second, the employee should complete a whole task, from beginning to end, rather than play a minor role in the big picture; finally, the employee should feel that her work has a significant impact on others. A manager who designs work that meets these conditions is likely to increase her employees' profits in the ultimate currency.

As I discussed in Chapter 6, work by Mihaly Csikszentmihalyi illustrates how a challenging task that is neither too difficult nor too easy leads to higher levels of engagement; a manager who is mindful of the benefits of engagement—for both the employee and the organization—will more likely assign work that challenges the employee to the right degree.

**TIME-IN** Think back to some of your favorite work experiences. What was it about the specific projects or the workplace that made the experience a positive one?

We cannot, though, simply hope that the right job or right employer will be handed to us. We have to actively seek and create meaning and pleasure in the workplace. Blaming others—our parents, our teachers, our boss, or the government—may yield sympathy but not happiness. The ultimate responsibility for finding the right job or creating the right conditions at work lies with us.

In some jobs it is possible to restructure work to meet the conditions necessary for the attainment of the ultimate currency. For example, we can experience flow by setting clear goals and challenging ourselves even when our job does not require that we do so. We can assume more responsibility and seek higher levels of involvement in work that we find interesting; we can take initiative and look for areas where we can contribute more to the organization, moving to a different department or getting involved in a new project. If, however, the setup of our job is such that it is impossible for us to feel interested and engaged, no matter how hard we try, then we might choose to look for an alternative source of income. While in some cases leaving our current workplace might not seem to be a feasible option, in most cases we can find an alternative—a workplace that, beyond the hard currency necessary for our basic material needs, will provide us with the ultimate currency.

Committing to change within the workplace or looking for a new job can be frightening. However, change is necessary if we are stuck in a job that supplies us with little beyond our material needs. Had we found ourselves in a job that did not afford us our basic material needs, we would do everything in our power to change our predicament. So why do we set lower standards for ourselves when the ultimate currency—when our own happiness—is at stake? What we need if we are to implement change in our lives is courage. And *courage is not about not having fear but about having fear and going ahead anyway.*

Hard currency and the ultimate currency are both necessary for our survival, and they need *not* be mutually exclusive. Moreover, because we often perform best at the things that we find most engaging, pursuing those activities that provide us meaning and pleasure could actually lead to more quantifiable success in the long run. We naturally work harder at the things that we care about and are interested in—that we are passionate about. Without passion, motivation wanes; with passion, motivation increases, and, over time, so does ability.

The investment we make in our work cannot be determined merely by what we stand to gain or lose financially. As the example of the emotionless robot illustrates, without having an emotional investment in our work, we ultimately lose interest. Emotions lead to motion—they are our fuel.

## Finding Our Calling

The psychologist Abraham Maslow once wrote that "the most beautiful fate, the most wonderful good fortune that can happen to any human being, is to be paid for doing that which he passionately loves to do." It is not always easy to discover what sort of work might yield this "good fortune" in the ultimate currency. Research examining the relation people have toward their work can help.

Psychologist Amy Wrzesniewski and her colleagues suggest that people experience their work in one of three ways: as a job, as a career, or as a calling.[2] A job is mostly perceived as a chore, with the focus being financial rewards rather than personal fulfillment. The person goes to work in the morning primarily because he feels that he has to rather than wants to. He has no real expectations from the job beyond the paycheck at the end of the week or month, and he mostly looks forward to Friday or to taking a vacation.

The person on a career path is primarily motivated by extrinsic factors, such as money and advancement—by power and prestige. She looks forward to the next promotion, to the next advancement up the hierarchy—from associate to tenured professor, from teacher to headmistress, from vice president to president, from assistant editor to editor in chief.

For a person experiencing his work as a calling, work is an end in itself. While the paycheck is certainly important and advancement is, too, he primarily works because he wants to. He is motivated by intrinsic reasons and experiences a sense of personal fulfillment; his goals are self-concordant. He is passionate about what he does and derives personal fulfillment from his work; he perceives it as a privilege rather than a chore.

**TIME-IN** Do you see your work as a job, a career, or a calling? Ask the same question about other work you have done in the past.

The way we are oriented toward work—whether we experience work as a job, a career, or a calling—has consequences for our well-being at work and in other areas. Wrzesniewski finds that "satisfaction with life and with work may be more dependent on how an employee sees his or her work than on income or occupational prestige."

It takes a conscious and concerted effort to find our calling, because we are usually encouraged to pursue what we do *well* rather than what we want to do. Most career advisers and job placement tests, for example, focus on our strengths rather than our passions. Questions such as "What am I good at?" are, of course, important in selecting our path, but we must ask them only after we have identified what gives us meaning and pleasure. When our first question is "What *can* I do?" we give priority to quantifiable currencies (money and the approval of others); when our first question is "What do I *want* to do?" (that is, "What gives me meaning and pleasure?"), our choice is driven by our pursuit of the ultimate currency.

## The Meaning, Pleasure, Strengths (MPS) Process

Finding the right work—work that corresponds to both our passions and our strengths—can be challenging. We can begin the process by asking these three crucial questions—"What gives me *meaning*?" "What gives me *pleasure*?" "What are my *strengths*?"—and noting the trends that emerge. Looking at the answers and identifying areas of overlap can help us determine what kind of work would make us happiest.[3]

Generating accurate answers to these questions requires more effort than simply jotting down whatever leaps to mind when, for instance, we try to think about what we find meaningful. Most of us have more or less ready-made answers to such questions; these answers are usually true but may stop short of representing the full range of experiences that we have found meaningful. We may need to spend time reflecting, thinking deeply to recall those moments in our lives when we felt a sense of true purpose.

We may also need to spend some time considering the answers to the three questions. The lists we generate may be long, and the way in which we phrase our answers may not make the areas of overlap immediately apparent.

## Using the MPS Process

Our lists will probably be messier and less straightforward than the following example, which is meant to show how the process works in its most basic form—how thinking about meaning, pleasure, and our strengths can lead us to more happiness and success.

Let's say I derive meaning from solving problems, writing, working with children, engaging in political activism, and music.

I enjoy sailing, cooking, reading, music, and being around children. My strengths are my sense of humor, my enthusiasm, my ability to relate to children, and my problem-solving skills.

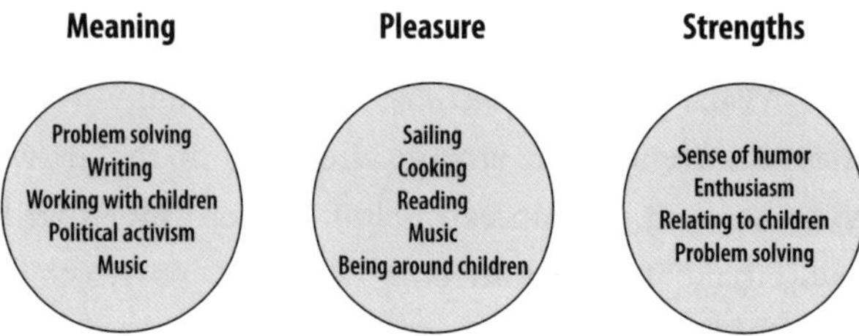


Which of the answers overlap?

In looking at the second diagram, I can see that working with children would give me meaning and pleasure, and I would be good at it. To figure out what specific jobs would be best for me, I would now take into consideration some other aspects of my personality and my life. For example, I am highly organized and like to plan my week's work in advance—therefore, I prefer to have a more structured daily schedule. I like to travel, and it would therefore be important for me to have a job that allows long breaks.

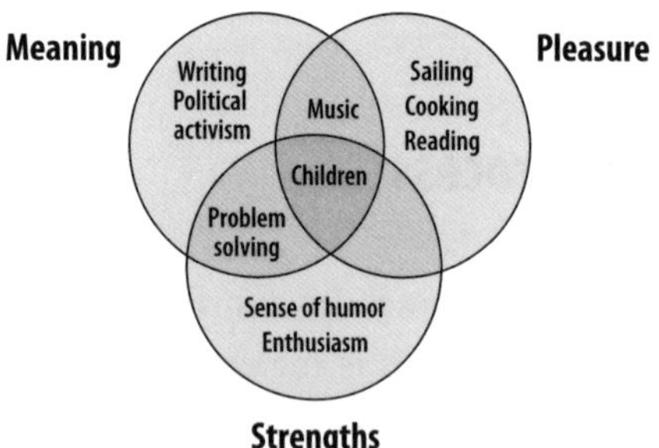


So what kind of work with children would provide a structured daily schedule and long breaks? What kind of work might involve or make the best use of my other passions and skills, such as my enthusiasm, my sense of humor, and my love of reading and problem solving? Taking all of these factors into account, I might consider becoming an English teacher. While the process may not have led me to the most financially remunerative job, it may have helped me to identify the work that is most profitable to me in the ultimate currency.

The MPS process can also help us make important decisions in other areas of our lives. When choosing a class in school, for example, we can look for an overlap between courses that would be meaningful for our future career, that we would enjoy, and that we would be good at.

A manager, too, can use the MPS process for the benefit of her staff and organization. Helping her employees identify and perform activities that they enjoy, find meaningful, and are good at will yield more commitment and better overall performance. The MPS process might even be useful for a manager selecting new employees. Not every workplace can satisfy the needs and tap the strengths of every person. It is important for the manager to create, from the outset, a fit between those she hires and what the workplace has to offer.

## Crafting Our Calling

The implicit assumption in the MPS process is that a person has a choice about where he works. But what if he has no choice or little choice? What if, because of external constraints, he cannot leave his current position or find work that meets the three criteria of meaning, pleasure, and strengths? Moreover, certain occupations or positions are more likely to draw out people's strengths and afford both meaning and pleasure. Working as a medical doctor, one could argue, lends itself more to meaning than work as a secondhand car dealer; similarly, Wrzesniewski's research illustrates that employees who are higher in the organizational hierarchy are more likely to experience their work as a calling.

But regardless of whether one is the CEO or a clerk, a physician or a salesperson, there is still much that a person can do to craft his work in a way that will maximize the yield in the ultimate currency—so that it is experienced more as a calling than as a job. In the words of Amy Wrzesniewski and Jane Dutton, "Even in the most restricted and routine jobs, employees can exert some influence on what is the essence of their work."

In research Wrzesniewski and Dutton conducted on hospital cleaners, one group of employees experienced their work as a job—as boring and meaningless—while the other group perceived the same work as engaging and meaningful. The second group of hospital cleaners crafted their work in creative ways. They engaged in more interactions with nurses, patients, and their visitors, taking it upon themselves to make the patients and hospital staff feel better. Generally, they saw their work in its broader context and actively imbued it with meaning: they were not merely removing the garbage and washing dirty linen but were contributing to patients' well-being and the smooth functioning of the hospital.

When it comes to generating the ultimate currency, how we *perceive* the work can matter more than the work itself. Hospital cleaners who recognize a simple truth, which is that their work makes a difference, are happier than doctors who don't experience their work as meaningful.

The researchers saw a similar trend among hairdressers, information technicians, nurses, and restaurant kitchen employees who created meaningful relationships with customers or with others in their organization. They found the same was true among engineers: those who saw themselves as teachers, team creators, and relationship builders felt they were contributing significantly to their companies' success, and thus related to their work more as a calling than as a job.

**TIME-IN** How can you craft your current work to have more meaning? What changes can you introduce?

## Focusing on Happiness

In *Zen and the Art of Motorcycle Maintenance*, Robert M. Pirsig writes, "The truth knocks on the door and you say, 'Go away, I'm looking for the truth' and so it goes away." We very often fail to recognize the rich sources of pleasure and meaning that are right in front of us in our work. The potential for happiness may be all around us, but if it goes unnoticed—if our focus is elsewhere and we fail to perceive it—we risk losing it. To turn a possibility into a *reality*, we first need to *realize* that the possibility exists.

Happiness is not merely contingent on what we do or where we are but on what we choose to perceive. There are people who are unhappy regardless of the work they do or the relationship they are in, and yet they continuously fool themselves into thinking that an external makeover will affect them internally.

Ralph Waldo Emerson was right: "To different minds, the same world is a hell, and a heaven." The exact same event can be perceived, and hence experienced, in very different ways by different people; what we choose to focus on largely determines whether or not we enjoy what we do—within a relationship, at school, and in the workplace. For example, an unhappy investment banker may learn to derive meaning and pleasure from her work if she chooses to focus on those aspects that are personally meaningful and pleasurable. If, however, like many people, she focuses primarily on the material rewards, she is less likely to sustain happiness. A change in perception can make a significant difference; as numerous hairdressers, hospital workers, and engineers so clearly demonstrate, we can find the treasure by focusing on it.

Hamlet's claim that "there is nothing either good or bad but thinking makes it so" is largely, but not entirely, accurate. The fact that what we choose to focus on—our perception—matters so much does not mean that just anybody can find happiness in any situation. For example, there are people who, regardless of their focus, will not derive meaning and pleasure from investment banking or from teaching. Of course there are also certain circumstances people find themselves in—stuck in an oppressive workplace, an oppressive relationship, or an oppressive country for that matter—that make the possibility of finding happiness extremely difficult. Happiness is a product of the external as well as of the internal, of what we choose to pursue as well as of what we choose to perceive.

Most of us can, and often do, find a job or a career in which we are relatively satisfied. But we can usually do better. To help us find our calling, we need to take the advice of my wise student Ebony Carter, who said, "Instead of focusing on what we can 'live with,' we should be thinking about what we can't live without." Finding a calling is about heeding the call of our inner voice. That call leads us to our calling; that voice guides us to our vocation.

## EXERCISES

### The Three-Question Process

Take the time to go through the MPS process described in greater depth earlier in this chapter. Write down your answers to the following questions, and then find the overlap among the responses.

**QUESTION 1:** What gives me meaning? In other words, what provides me with a sense of purpose?

**QUESTION 2:** What gives me pleasure? In other words, what do I enjoy doing?

**QUESTION 3:** What are my strengths? In other words, what am I good at?

Going through this process can help you identify your path on the macro level (what your life calling is) as well as the micro level (what you would like your day-to-day activities to look like). While the two are interconnected, it is more difficult, and therefore may take much more courage, to introduce the macro-level change—such as leaving one's work or the security of a known path. Micro-level changes, such as putting aside two weekly hours to practice one's hobby, are easier to introduce—and yet may still yield high dividends in the ultimate currency.

## Crafting Your Work

Short of a life-changing move, one way of enhancing the quality of our lives is to introduce new activities that are meaningful and pleasurable and that we are good at. Another way is to mine what we are already doing for the ultimate currency. And we usually do not need to dig very deep to find the treasure.

Our prejudice against work, or a narrow-minded perspective of the kind of work that can be meaningful, often makes us miss the truth—which is that the potential for happiness is all around us. This exercise can help identify and exploit the hidden treasures.

Describe in detail what you do during a typical day or two. Draw on the timeline you created as part of the "Mapping Your Life" exercise in Chapter 3 (or make a new timeline, specifically for work). Look at the description and ask yourself the following two questions. First, can you change some of your routines at work—incorporate more activities that are meaningful and/or pleasurable while you reduce the amount of work that you find uninspiring? Second, and regardless of whether you are able to introduce actual changes, ask yourself what potential meaning and pleasure already exist in what you do. Think about the hospital cleaners or hairdressers or engineers who were able to craft their work in ways that provided them with more of the ultimate currency. They did not change anything fundamental about their work or their workplace. But by highlighting certain elements of their work—like the potential inherent in their daily interactions with others—they increased the meaning and pleasure, and thus the happiness, they experienced at work.

Now, based on your answers to these questions, rewrite your "job description" into a "calling description." Write the description in a way that might entice others to apply for this job, to see it as desirable—not by misrepresenting it in any way, but by highlighting the potential pleasure and meaning that can be derived from it. How we perceive our work, how we describe it to ourselves and to others, can make a significant difference in terms of how we experience it.[4]

8

# Happiness in Relationships

**All who would win joy must share it; happiness was born a twin.**

*—Lord Byron*

Ed Diener and Martin Seligman, two of the leading positive psychologists, studied "very happy people" and compared them to those who were less happy. The only external factor that distinguished the two groups was the presence of "rich and satisfying social relationships." Spending meaningful time with friends, family, or romantic partners was necessary (though not by itself sufficient) for happiness.

Having people about whom we care and who care about us to share our lives with—to share the events and thoughts and feelings in our lives—intensifies our experience of meaning, consoles us in our pain, deepens our sense of delight in the world. Intimate friendships, according to seventeenth-century philosopher Francis Bacon, "redoubleth joys, and cutteth griefs in half." Without friendship, writes Aristotle, no happiness is possible.

While relationships in general are important for the ultimate currency, romantic relationships reign supreme. Summarizing the research on well-being, David Myers acknowledges that "there are few stronger predictions of happiness than a close, nurturing, equitable, intimate, lifelong companionship with one's best friend." There is no other topic that is written about more (in poetry, fiction, or nonfiction) or discussed more (in cafés, schools, online, or on the couch) than romantic love—the passionate attachment between two people. There is also no other topic as deeply misunderstood.

**TIME-IN** Think about the people who are closest to you. Are you spending as much time as you would like with them? If not, can you do something about it?

## Unconditional Love

One afternoon, a few weeks after winning the Israeli squash championship, I turned to my mother and, with the earnestness that only a self-important sixteen-year-old can muster, said, "I want women to want me for who I am, not for being the national champion." I am not entirely sure how much I was expressing a true concern (given the scarcity in Israel of squash courts, players, and, alas, fans) and how much I was driven by false modesty—imitating the rich and famous who complain of how hard it is to find someone to love them for who they "really" are. In truth, I was not much worried about being wanted for who I was; I simply wanted to be wanted.

Whatever my actual motivation for raising this issue might have been, my mother responded to it as seriously as she did to all the other grave concerns I seemed to have in those days. She said, "Your being the national champion *is* a reflection of who you are, of, among other things, your passion and dedication." As my mother understood the situation, winning the championship merely made certain qualities more visible. The external attracted more attention to the internal.

It took me years to grasp that what my mother meant by being loved for who we are differed from my own nebulous understanding of this concept. What does it mean to be wanted or loved for "who we really are"? To put it another way, what are we talking about when we talk about *unconditional love*, a phrase we throw around in the bedroom, the children's room, the classroom? Do we mean that we want someone to love us for no reason? To love us no matter what? Are we saying that love needs no justification?

Talking about love simply as a feeling, as an emotion or a state independent of reason, is reductive. Love cannot last without a rational foundation: just as positive emotions are insufficient for lasting happiness (the hedonist cannot sustain happiness because there is no meaning in his life), so strong feelings, in and of themselves, are insufficient to sustain love. When a man falls in love with a woman, he does so for certain conscious or unconscious *reasons*. He may *feel* that he just loves her "for who she is" but not be sure what he means by that; when asked to articulate why he loves her, he might respond, "I don't know, I just do." We are taught that falling in love with someone is about following our heart, not our mind—that love, by definition, is inexplicable, mystical, beyond reason. However, if it really is love that we feel, we do feel it for a reason. These reasons might not be conscious and accessible, but they nevertheless exist.

If, then, there are actual reasons for loving someone, if there are certain *conditions* under which we fall in love, can there be such a thing as unconditional love? Or is the idea of unconditional love fundamentally unreasonable? It depends on whether or not the characteristics we love in someone are manifestations of that person's core self.

## The Core Self

The core self comprises our deepest and most stable characteristics—our character. It comprises the actual principles by which we live, which are not necessarily synonymous with the ones we claim to follow. Because we cannot observe a core self directly, the only way for us to know a person's character is through its manifestations, through the person's behavior, which *is* observable.

A person who is empathetic, assiduous, patient, and enthusiastic—whose core self comprises these characteristics—might establish an intervention program for underprivileged children. The success or failure of the program, which is contingent on any number of external factors, may have nothing to do with who she is; it is the internal characteristics that led her to start the program that are part of her core self. Her behavior (starting the program) reflects her core self, whereas the outcome of her behavior (whether or not the program succeeds) does not. If someone loved her unconditionally, he would, of course, be delighted by the program's success and saddened by its failure; either way, though, his feelings toward *her* would not change because her core self would not have changed.

To be loved for our wealth, power, or fame is to be loved conditionally; to be loved for our steadfastness, intensity, or warmth is to be loved unconditionally.

**TIME-IN** What characteristics make up your core self?

## The Circle of Happiness

The psychologist Donald W. Winnicott observed that children playing in close proximity to their mothers display higher levels of creativity in their games than those who are farther away. Children are highly creative as long as they are within a certain radius of their mothers, inside a *circle of creativity*, of sorts. The circle of creativity is a space in which children can take risks and try things out, fall and stand up again, fail and succeed—because they feel secure and safe in the presence of a person who loves them unconditionally.

Because adults are capable of higher levels of abstraction than children, we do not always have to be physically near our loved ones to be within their circle of creativity. The knowledge that we are loved unconditionally creates a psychological space of safety and security.

Unconditional love creates a parallel *circle of happiness*—in which we are encouraged to pursue those things that are meaningful and pleasurable for us. We experience the freedom to follow our passions—whether in art, banking, teaching, or gardening—regardless of prestige or success. Unconditional love is the foundation of a happy relationship.

If someone truly loves me, he or she, more than anything else, would want me to express my core self and would draw out those qualities that make me who I really am.

## Meaning and Pleasure in Love

While unconditional love is necessary for a happy relationship, it is, in and of itself, insufficient. Just as meaning and pleasure, future and present benefit, are essential for sustained happiness at work and at school, so are they essential for a happy relationship.

Couples who get together primarily for some future gain—because being together will help them get ahead in some way, socially or financially, for example—are in rat-race relationships.

So are those couples who justify working hard and spending little time with each other on the grounds that they are doing so for the sake of the relationship—to ensure a secure and happy future together. While it is sometimes necessary to forgo present benefit for the sake of future goals, spending too much time living for the future will ultimately lead to the relationship's failure.

At the other extreme is the hedonist, who enters into and evaluates a relationship primarily on the basis of how much pleasure it provides. Mistaking pleasure for happiness, the hedonist in a relationship mistakes lust for love. The hedonist's pleasure inevitably fades, though, because without a meaningful foundation to the relationship that goes beyond immediate gratification, it is impossible to sustain happiness.

And the nihilist? He might decide to get married because that is the "right" thing to do or because it's what all his friends are doing. He neither expects nor gets much from the relationship and instead drifts aimlessly and unhappily alongside his partner.

**TIME-IN** Think about one or two of your past relationships—either romantic relationships or friendships. What quadrant did they fall under? Did the nature of these relationships change over time?

## Love and Sacrifice

Even people who believe that happiness might be attainable with the right person may resign themselves to an unhappy relationship out of a sense of duty toward their partners, their children, or the institution of marriage. They believe, mistakenly, that sacrifice is synonymous with virtue, failing to recognize that staying in the relationship for the sake of the other will lead them both to frustration and unhappiness. Over time, the person sacrificing will resent his partner for depriving him of the meaning or pleasure he might find elsewhere. His partner, in turn, will be miserable knowing that he remains with her because he *has to*, not because he *wants to*, and she, too, will lose any meaning or pleasure she might have derived from the relationship.

Even within a relationship in which partners love each other and want to be together, happiness can be undermined by the belief that sacrifice is synonymous with love—that the greater the sacrifice, the deeper the love.

It is important to note that standing by one's partner in a time of need is not sacrifice; when we love someone, we often feel that helping that person is helping ourselves. As Nathaniel Branden notes, "This is the great complement of love: that our self-interest expands to encompass our partner."

When I speak of sacrifice here, I am speaking of a person renouncing something that is essential to his or her happiness. For example, a woman permanently giving up work she loves and cannot find elsewhere so that her husband can take a job abroad *is* sacrificing—because if her work is fundamental to her core self, if it is part of her calling, then abandoning it is detrimental to her happiness. The same woman taking a week off from work because she wants to help her husband with an important project is not necessarily sacrificing—she may not be compromising her core self in any way and thus may not be compromising her happiness. Moreover, because her happiness is intertwined with his, because each of them is happier when the other is happy, helping him is also helping herself.

There is no easy way to distinguish between behavior that is sacrificial, and hence destructive to the long-term success of the relationship, and behavior that is conducive to the growth of the relationship. The only way to begin to sort out the harmful from the beneficial is by evaluating the relationship, as a whole, in the currency of happiness.

A relationship is a transaction in the ultimate currency. Like every transaction, the more profitable a relationship is for *both* people, the more likely it is to flourish. When one of the partners is shortchanged in the ultimate currency—when she is constantly giving up meaning and pleasure so that he can have more of it—both partners end up less happy in the long run. In order to feel satisfied within a relationship, we have to feel that the transaction is equitable.

Psychologist Elaine Hatfield, who studies relationships, shows that people do not like being "overpaid" or "underpaid" in a relationship. People feel more content, and relationships are more likely to prosper, when both partners see the relationship as equitable. This of course does not mean that both partners must earn similar salaries; the relationship's equity is measured in the ultimate currency. While compromise is a natural and healthy part of any relationship, while at different times each partner will forgo some meaning or pleasure for the sake of the other, *overall* the relationship must profit both partners—both must be happier for being together.

**TIME-IN** What are some ways in which you and your partner (or friend) help one another become happier? What other things can the two of you do to help the relationship become a richer source of the ultimate currency?

## To Be Known Rather than Validated

In the United States alone, approximately 40 percent of marriages end up in divorce; this statistic does not bode well for our capacity for long-term romance, especially when we consider that the 60 percent of couples who stay together are not necessarily flourishing within the relationship. Do these statistics suggest that we are not designed for long-term, monogamous relationships? No. No more than the statistics on depression imply that we are doomed to a life of unhappiness.

While divorce is at times the best option—not all couples are compatible or have the potential to become compatible—very often the cause of separation stems from a basic misunderstanding of what love is and what it entails. Many people mistake pure sexual desire (lust) for true love, but while sexual attraction is necessary for romantic love, it is not sufficient on its own. A relationship founded primarily on lust cannot last for long. No matter how "objectively" attractive one's partner is or how much "subjective" attraction exists between the partners, the initial excitement, the purely physical attraction, wears off. Novelty excites our senses, the "exotic becomes erotic"[1]; in contrast, after a while a live-in partner becomes familiar.

But while familiarity can lead to decreased physical excitement, growing very familiar with your partner, getting to truly *know* her, can also lead to higher levels of intimacy—and thus to both deeper love and better sex.

In his book *Passionate Marriage*, sex therapist David Schnarch challenges the view, prevalent in his field, that sex and passion are simply reducible to biological drives. If sex is indeed just that, then there is little hope for sustained, long-term passionate relationships. However, over decades of work with couples, Schnarch has demonstrated that sex can get better if we focus on knowing, and being known by, our partner.

Schnarch says that to cultivate genuine intimacy the focus in a relationship must shift from the desire to be *validated*—seeking approval and praise—to the desire to be *known*. In order for the love and passion in a relationship to grow over time, both partners must be willing to be known, and this means gradually disclosing their innermost selves—their desires, fears, fantasies, dreams—even when those do not show them in the most favorable light. Over the years, partners can create an increasingly comprehensive "love map" of one another's world—a deeper and deeper understanding of their partner's values, passions, concerns, and hopes.[2]

The process of knowing and being know is, potentially, never-ending, as there is always more that can be revealed, always more that can be discovered. The relationship, therefore, is far more likely to remain interesting, exciting, stimulating. Being together—whether talking over a coffee, caring for children, or making love—becomes so much more meaningful and pleasurable when our focus shifts from validation to knowing and being known.

**TIME-IN** Think of ways in which you can help your partner get to know you better. Think of ways in which you can get to know your partner better.

## Cultivating over Finding

Many people believe that the key to a successful relationship is finding the right partner. In fact, however, the most important and challenging component of a happy relationship is not finding the one right person—I do not believe that there is just one right person for each of us—but rather *cultivating the one chosen relationship*.

The erroneous belief that places finding over cultivating can, at least in part, be attributed to the silver screen. Many movies are about the search for love, the trials and tribulations that two people go through until they find each other. Toward the end of the movie, the lovers get together, kiss passionately, and then live happily ever after—or so we assume. The problem is that *movies end where love begins*. It's the living happily ever after that poses the greatest challenge; it's after the sun sets that difficulties often rise.

The mistaken notion that finding love guarantees eternal bliss leads partners to neglect the journey—the day-to-day issues, activities, and events that shape the relationship. Would anyone seriously entertain the notion that once he found his dream job, the ideal workplace, he would no longer need to work hard? Such an approach would inevitably lead to failure. It is no different when it comes to relationships: the real, hard work begins after we fall in love. In the context of a relationship, the hard work is about cultivating intimacy.

We cultivate intimacy by knowing and being known. We can then deepen our intimacy by acting on our knowledge of one another—engaging in activities that are meaningful and pleasurable to ourselves as well as to our partner. Over time, as we get to know one another and spend time together engaged in activities that we care about most, we build a foundation that can weather inevitable storms as well as provide fertile ground for love, and happiness, to blossom.

## EXERCISES

### A Letter of Gratitude

In his positive psychology class, Martin Seligman encourages his students to write gratitude letters and make gratitude visits to people they care about. This simple exercise, which I used in my class, often has profound effects on both the writer and the receiver—and on the relationship.

A gratitude letter is not just a thank-you note. It is a thoughtful examination of the meaning and pleasure that you derive from the relationship; it describes particular experiences and shared dreams, and whatever else in the relationship is a source of joy.

Relationship expert John Gottman is able to predict the success of a relationship based on how partners describe their past. If partners focus on the happy aspects of their time together, if they remember the past fondly, the relationship is much more likely to thrive. Focusing on meaningful and pleasurable experiences—in the past and the present—fortifies the connection and improves the relationship overall. A gratitude letter highlights the positive elements of the relationship—past, present, and future—and thereby accentuates them.

Make it a ritual to write at least one or two gratitude letters a month to people you care about—a lover, a family member, a dear friend.

## Sentence Completion

Following are some sentence stems that can help you find greater love within a relationship, romantic or otherwise. Some of the stems are relevant for people who are in a relationship, others for people in search of a relationship; most are relevant for both.

Being in love means . . .  
To be a better friend . . .  
To be a better partner . . .  
To bring 5 percent more happiness to my romantic relationship . . .  
To bring 5 percent more happiness to my friendships . . .  
To bring love to my life . . .  
I am becoming aware . . .  
If I take more responsibility for fulfilling my desires . . .  
If I let go and allow myself to experience what love feels like . . .

Part 3

# Meditations on HAPPINESS

9

# First Meditation: Self-Interest and Benevolence

**Don't ask yourself what the world needs, ask yourself what makes you come alive. And then go and do that. Because what the world needs is people who have come alive.**

—*Harold Whitman*

Teaching is my calling. I teach executives in organizations, students in college, and at-risk youth in inner cities. I teach because it makes me happy, because it affords me present and future benefit, pleasure and meaning. I teach because I *want to* (because I love it), not because I feel I *have to* (out of some abstract sense of duty to others).

In other words, I am no altruist. The ultimate reason that I do anything—whether it is spending time with my friends or doing work for charity—is that it makes me happy. The ultimate currency, in theory and in practice, is the end toward which all of my actions lead.

The idea that our actions should be guided by self-interest, by our own happiness, can make some people uneasy. The source of their unease is a belief—explicit or implicit—in the morality of duty.

Immanuel Kant, the influential eighteenth-century German philosopher, tells us that for an act to have moral worth, it must be undertaken out of a sense of duty. When we act out of self-interest, then, we preclude the possibility of our action being a moral one. According to Kant, if a person helps another because he feels inclined to do so—because it makes him happy—what he does has no moral value.

Most of those philosophies and religions that advocate self-sacrifice as the foundation of morality, as Kant does, assume that acting in one's self-interest inevitably leads to acting against the interests of others—that if we do not fight our selfish inclinations, we will hurt others and disregard their needs.

What this worldview fails to acknowledge, however, is that we do not need to make a choice between helping others and helping ourselves. They are not mutually exclusive possibilities. In fact, as the philosopher Ralph Waldo Emerson explains, "It is one of the most beautiful compensations of this life that no man can sincerely try to help another without helping himself." Helping oneself and helping others are inextricably intertwined: the more we help others, the happier we become, and the happier we become, the more inclined we are to help others.

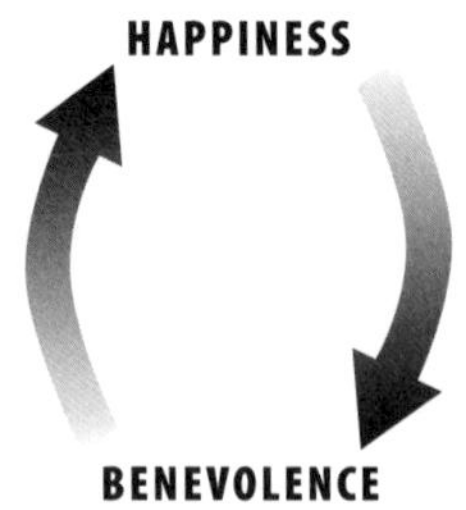

**TIME-IN** Think back to a time you helped someone. Try to reexperience the emotions you felt.

Contributing to other people's happiness provides us with meaning and pleasure, which is why helping others is one of the essential components of a happy life. Of course it is important to keep in mind the distinction between helping others and living for others' happiness. If we do not make the pursuit of our own happiness a priority, we are hurting ourselves and, by extension, our inclination to help others. An unhappy person is less likely to be benevolent—and that leads to further unhappiness.

Research by Barbara Fredrickson suggests that positive emotions broaden the scope of our attention. When we're happy, then, we are more likely to see beyond our narrow, inward-looking, and self-centered perspective and focus on others' needs and wants. Research by Alice Isen and Jennifer George illustrates that we are more likely to help others when we feel good.

We often enhance our happiness to the greatest extent when we pursue activities that provide us with meaning and pleasure *and* that help others. When making choices, we first need to ask ourselves what would make us happy *independent* of how much it might contribute to the happiness of others. We must then ask ourselves whether what we want to do would deprive others of their ability to pursue their own happiness—because if it would, we would be undermining our happiness. Our empathic inclinations, our innate sense of justice, inevitably lead us to pay the price in the ultimate currency when we hurt people.[1]

For those who subscribe to the morality of duty, finding meaning—leading a moral life—necessitates sacrifice. Sacrifice, by definition, is not pleasurable (if it were, it would no longer be sacrifice). The morality of duty, therefore, pits meaning and pleasure against each other.

Happiness is not about sacrifice, about a trade-off between present and future benefit, between meaning and pleasure, between helping ourselves and helping others. It is about synthesis, about creating a life in which all of the elements essential to happiness are in harmony.

## EXERCISE

### Meditating on Benevolence

Follow the instructions in the exercise "Meditating on Happiness" at the end of Chapter 2 and try to enter a calm and relaxed state.

Think back to a time when you behaved benevolently toward someone else and felt appreciated for it. In your mind's eye, see the person's response to your act. Savor it. Experience your own feelings; allow them to materialize inside you. As you see the other person and experience your own feelings, break the artificial divide that currently exists between helping oneself and helping others.

Now think about a future opportunity. It could be sharing an idea with a friend, giving flowers to a loved one, reading to your child, or donating to a cause you believe in. Experience the deep happiness that can come with each act of generosity.

If you have started a regular meditation practice, as recommended in Chapter 2, once in a while incorporate meditation on benevolence—in addition to meditating on happiness.

10

# Second Meditation: Happiness Boosters

**Fill your life with as many moments and experiences of joy and passion as you humanly can. Start with one experience and build on it.**

—*Marcia Wieder*

In a perfect world, we would be able to engage in meaningful and pleasurable activities all day, every day. In our world, for most people, that is not possible. A single parent does not always have the luxury of leaving a well-paying job she dislikes for more gratifying work that pays less. Getting food on her children's table and providing them with shelter and a decent education are her top priorities.

Others who have more choice than the single parent can justifiably forgo pleasure in the short term for larger future rewards. A fresh college graduate, for instance, may want to acquire business experience working as an investment banker for two years, even though she does not enjoy spending fourteen hours a day in front of the computer. As long as she keeps in mind that happiness is the highest on the hierarchy of goals and she does not fall into the trap of the rat racer—postponing gratification indefinitely—staying the two years may be the right thing for her.

Then, most people, rich or poor, young or old, go through spells of happiness drought. I have not met many students who enjoy exam period; and even in the most engaging workplaces, some projects are less interesting than others. Whether it is out of necessity or by choice, for most of us there are periods when much of what we do does not afford us satisfaction. Fortunately, this does not mean that we need to resign ourselves to unhappiness during these times—be it for the month of exams or a dull period at work, for two years while we gain work experience or the twenty-two years during which our children need our financial support.

Research by Kennon Sheldon and Linda Houser-Marko shows that pursuing self-concordant goals—engaging in activities that are personally meaningful—impacts our experience in other areas, not directly related to these activities: "Those people who can identify sets of goals that well represent their implicit interests and values are indeed able to function more efficiently, flexibly, and integratively across all areas of their lives."[1] The confidence, the passion, the sense of fulfillment they gained from such experiences spilled over to other areas of their lives.

Meaningful and pleasurable activities can function like a candle in a dark room—and just as it takes a small flame or two to light up an entire physical space, one or two happy experiences during an otherwise uninspiring period can transform our general state. I call these brief but transforming experiences *happiness boosters*—activities, lasting anywhere from a few minutes to a few hours, that provide us with both meaning and pleasure, both future and present benefit.

Happiness boosters can inspire and invigorate us, acting as both a motivational *pull* and a motivational *push*. For the single parent, a happiness booster in the form of a meaningful outing with her children over the weekend can change her overall experience of life—including the hours spent at work. The outing can motivate her and pull her through the week, giving her something to look forward to when she gets up for work in the morning. The same happiness booster can then energize her, providing her the push she needs by recharging her motivational stores for the following week. For the young investment banker, two hours a week helping her community center with its finances and spending one evening a week with friends can help her endure, and even enjoy, the two years of hard and largely unfulfilling work.

I recently met a partner in a top consulting firm. Now in his fifties, he no longer enjoys consulting, but at the same time he does not want to leave his profession and give up the lifestyle to which he and his family have grown accustomed. However, he was able to reduce his workload sufficiently to introduce some happiness boosters. Currently, he spends at least two evenings each week with his family, plays tennis twice a week (or works out in the gym if he's traveling), and spends more than three hours each week reading for pleasure. He also joined the board of his high school, where he feels that he can contribute in a meaningful way to the education of the next generation. Just as he does not miss a meeting with a client, he does not miss a meeting with his family, the school board, or himself. While in an ideal world he would be spending his working hours doing something he is passionate about, he still is happier than he has been for a long time.

**TIME-IN** What are your happiness boosters? What brief activities can rejuvenate you by providing you with both meaning and pleasure?

## Introducing Change

Happiness boosters can also help in the difficult process of change; habits often persist even if we do recognize the need for a new or altered course of action. Seventeenth-century British poet John Dryden said that "we first make our habits and then our habits make us." And if we are in the habit of living as rat racers—having been conditioned to do so from an early age—it is extremely difficult to disembark from the treadmill. Similarly, a hedonistic lifestyle may be destructive, but it can also be addictive, difficult to give up. An easier, more manageable way of bringing about change in the quality of life is through the gradual introduction of happiness boosters.

Introducing relatively brief experiences of meaning and pleasure is less threatening than overhauling an entire life and will therefore meet with less resistance—both from the person trying to change as well as from his family, colleagues, and friends. Before making a career move from investing to teaching, a person may choose to volunteer once a week in an after-school program, in order to be certain that teaching does, indeed, provide both future and present benefit. Alternatively, a person who is not happy working in education and wants to pursue a career in the money market may want to spend some of his free time playing around with stocks to assure himself, as much as is possible, that the change he has been imagining will, in fact, make him happier. By affording the opportunity for trial and error, with minimal risk, happiness boosters can help us hone in on what we want to do most.

## The Value of Free Time

Ideally, we want our entire day to be filled with happy experiences. This kind of life is not always attainable, though, and it might be that we need to wait until evenings or weekends to pursue activities that provide present and future benefit. One of the common mistakes people make is that in their free time they choose passive hedonism over an active pursuit of happiness. At the end of a hard day at work or in school, they opt to do nothing or to vegetate in front of the television screen rather than engage in activities that are both pleasurable and meaningful. Soon after they engage in their mindless activity, they fall asleep, which further reinforces their belief that when they complete their daily chores they are too tired to do anything challenging.

If instead of doing nothing when we come home from work we turn to our hobbies or other activities that challenge us, that we enjoy and that we care about, we are more likely to get a second wind and replenish our emotional bank. As the educator Maria Montessori has written, "To devote oneself to an agreeable task is restful." Happiness boosters, rather than enervating us, lead to ascending levels of energy.

## EXERCISE

### Boosting Our Happiness

Generate a list of happiness boosters that you can then pursue throughout your week. These can include "general" boosters that you can do as a matter of routine (spending time with one's family and friends, pleasure reading, and so on) as well as "exploratory" boosters that can help you find out whether to introduce a more significant change to your life (volunteering at a school once a week, for instance). Enter the boosters into your daily planner and, if possible, create rituals around them.

11

# Third Meditation: Beyond the Temporary High

**Happiness depends upon ourselves.**

—*Aristotle*

Tami, my wife, distinguishes between *height* and *depth* as they relate to happiness: "The height element refers to the fluctuations in our levels of well-being, the highs and lows we experience; the depth refers to that part of our well-being that is stable, to our base level of happiness." For example, the sense of relief a rat racer experiences after attaining a goal is a transitory high; it does not necessarily affect his overall level of happiness. The depth of our happiness is like the roots of a tree—providing the foundation, the constant element of our well-being. The height of our happiness is like the leaves—beautiful, coveted, and yet ephemeral, changing and withering with the seasons.

The question that many philosophers and psychologists have asked is whether the depth of our happiness can be changed or whether we are predestined to experience highs and lows around a fixed level of the ultimate currency.

In his classic work, *Psycho-Cybernetics*, Maxwell Maltz writes about an internal thermostat-like mechanism that controls and checks our happiness level. For most people, the level at which this internal mechanism is set does not change much throughout life—deviations, highs or lows, are quickly corrected and we return to our base level of happiness. Of course, we are delighted when good things happen to us (when, for example, we win a lottery or secure our dream job) and are saddened when things do not go as we would wish (when we experience loss). These emotions, though, usually last for only a short time; win or lose, the depth of our happiness does not change, and we soon recover our familiar sense of well-being.

The famous Minnesota twin studies, in which identical twins reared apart were shown to have similar personality traits, coupled with research that suggests the existence of a base level of well-being, have led some psychologists to argue that our quota of happiness is determined by our genes or by early experiences—that, as adults, we have no control over how happy we are. The psychologists David Lykken and Auke Tellegan, for example, concluded that "it may be that trying to be happier is as futile as trying to be taller and is therefore counterproductive."

Such claims, which suggest that our portion of the ultimate currency is predetermined, are misleading. They ignore much evidence that demonstrates that a person's base level of happiness can change, that a person can become happier. A gifted psychotherapist, for example, can help people find more of the ultimate currency. Sometimes an encounter—with a friend or a book, a piece of art or an idea—can change a person's life for the better.

**TIME-IN** What experiences or people in your life have contributed to your happiness?

While there is some genetic component to our happiness—some people are born with a happier disposition than others—our genes define a range not a set point. Grumpy may not be able to cultivate the same view of life that Happy enjoys, and a natural-born whiner may not be able to transform himself into a Pollyanna, but we all can become significantly happier. And most people fall far short of their happiness potential.

In a review of the literature on happiness, Sonja Lyubomirsky, Kennon Sheldon, and David Schkade illustrate how a person's level of happiness is primarily determined by three factors: "a genetically determined set point for happiness, happiness-relevant circumstantial factors, and happiness-relevant activities and practices." While we have no control over our genetic predisposition and sometimes little influence over the circumstances in which we find ourselves, we usually have considerably more control over the kind of activities and practices that we pursue. This third category, according to Lyubomirsky and her colleagues, "offers the best opportunities for sustainably increasing happiness." Pursuing meaningful and pleasurable activities can significantly raise our levels of well-being.

## The Error of the Average

Psychologists who argue that the depth of our happiness is fixed make the "error of the average"—they derive their conclusions from what most people do while ignoring those who don't fit the norm. Even in the Minnesota twin studies, not all identical twins enjoy identical levels of happiness; in other studies, not all people—100 percent of participants—return to their base level of happiness after each event.

The average is indicative of a trend, not of a necessity or of a universal truth. Often, it is those outside the norm, the exceptional ones, who point to the truth of what is possible. That some people, throughout their lives, enjoy progressively higher levels of happiness indicates that it is possible to reset the thermostat. The question we should be concerned with, therefore, is not whether or not it is possible to become happier but rather how to do it. This book provides some, but not all, of the answers. Those who shift their focus from material goods and prestige to the ultimate currency will raise their base level of well-being; those who actively seek present and future benefit will be happier in the long run.

The argument that the depth element of our happiness is immutable is not only misleading, it is also potentially detrimental. A person who is led to believe that, no matter what she does, her share of the ultimate currency is predetermined is less likely to act and try to better her predicament. Therefore, her belief that her happiness level is fixed and cannot be changed could become a self-fulfilling prophecy. Worse, the belief that she cannot improve her lot, though predicated on a false theory, might lead her to helplessness and despair—to nihilism.

While we are born with a certain natural disposition (along the Happy-Grumpy continuum) and there are events over which we have little control, we do have some control over how we spend our time. According to Daniel Kahneman, "Time-use may be the determinant of well-being that is the most susceptible to improvement."[1] Most people fall far short of their potential for happiness because they misuse precious time—racing like rats, seeking mindless hedonism, or resigning themselves to nihilism. Within time lies the potential for an impoverished life or for a life of fulfillment; properly used, time becomes the keeper of the ultimate treasure.

Our pursuit of the ultimate currency can be a never-ending process of flourishing and growth; there is no limit to how much happiness we can attain. By pursuing work, education, and relationships that yield both meaning and pleasure, we become progressively happier—experiencing not just an ephemeral high that withers with the leaves but lasting happiness with deep and stable roots.

## EXERCISE

### Appreciative Inquiry

In the 1980s, David Cooperrider and his colleagues introduced a simple yet revolutionary approach to change that has since helped numerous individuals and organizations learn and grow.[2] Rather than focusing on what doesn't work, on the problem areas—as most intervention programs or consultants do—Appreciative Inquiry focuses on what has worked or does work. To "appreciate" means to recognize the value of something and also to increase its value (money in the bank can appreciate). By inquiring into positive past experiences, we can learn from them and then apply our learning to present and future situations.

You can do this exercise on your own, though it is better to do it with a partner or in a small group. If you're doing it with others, take turns telling one another what has made you happier in the past—ten years ago, last month, or earlier today. It could be a meal, an evening with your family, a specific project at work, or a concert. What, specifically, was it that made you feel good? Was it the connection you felt to other people? Was it the fact that you were challenged? Was it a sense of awe that you experienced?

After inquiring into the positive aspects of your experiences—whether on your own or with the help of others—ask yourself how you can take what you have learned from your best past and apply it toward creating a better future. Commit yourself, in writing and to those doing the exercise with you, to activities that you believe will make you happier.

12

# Fourth Meditation: Letting Our Light Shine

**Most people are about as happy as they make up their minds to be.**

*—Abraham Lincoln*

Our capacity for the pursuit of happiness is a gift of nature. No person, no religion, no ideology, no government has the right to take it away from us. Enlightened nations set up political structures—constitutions, courts of law, armies—to protect our right to freely pursue happiness. Yet nothing external can protect us from what I have come to believe is one of the greatest impediments we face in our pursuit of the ultimate currency—our feeling that we are somehow unworthy of happiness.

Understanding the theory of happiness that I have presented here—our need for both pleasure and meaning in our lives—is not enough to guarantee sustained happiness. If, at some level, we feel unworthy of being happy, we will find ways to limit our capacity for happiness. We may overlook or fail to appreciate potential sources of the ultimate currency, we may focus our energy on activities that make us unhappy, we may trivialize the happiness we do experience, or we may constantly remind ourselves of all the things we are not happy about.

Many people choose to do work they dislike when they could easily find work that would pay them well in the ultimate currency; many people resign themselves to being either alone or in an unhappy relationship rather than making the effort to find a person with whom to share their lives or to cultivate their existing relationship. Some people have jobs that provide them with present and future benefit yet still manage to find reasons to be unhappy at work; some people find meaning and pleasure in a relationship and then find ways to sabotage it. I have done all of these things, and more, to undermine my own happiness.

Why would anyone actively deprive himself of happiness? In her book *A Return to Love*, Marianne Williamson says:

> Our deepest fear is not that we are inadequate. Our deepest fear is that we are powerful beyond measure. It is our light, not our darkness, that most frightens us. We ask ourselves who am I to be brilliant, gorgeous, talented and fabulous? Actually, who are you not to be?

Who are we *not* to be happy? Why does the light frighten us more than the darkness? Why do we think that we are unworthy of happiness?

There are external and internal factors, cultural and psychological biases, that conspire against our being happy. On the most fundamental level, the idea that we have the *right* to be happy, that individual happiness is a noble and worthy pursuit, is censured and vilified by many ideologies. Many of the cultural legacies that have been passed down to us presume that we are inherently evil, that we are driven by aggression and the death instinct—that our lives unredeemed by the civilizing forces of our culture would be, in the words of the philosopher Thomas Hobbes, "solitary, poor, nasty, brutish, and short." Who would deem these creatures deserving of happiness? With such views so deeply ingrained in our culture, it is no wonder we feel ourselves more suited to the darkness than the light.

The assumptions that hold us back are not only the ones we have internalized from our predecessors. Many of us have limitations that are self-generated. When we do not feel that we are worthy of happiness, we cannot possibly feel worthy of the good things in our lives, the things that bring us happiness. Because we do not believe we actually deserve them, that they could really be ours, we fear their loss. This fear causes actual behaviors that lead to a self-fulfilling prophecy: our fear of loss creates actual loss; our feelings of being unworthy of happiness in fact lead to unhappiness.

A person who fears loss may protect himself by ensuring that he has nothing to lose. When we are happy, we have a lot to lose. To avoid the devastation of a loss, we exclude the possibility of any gain. We fear the worst and thus, from the outset, deprive ourselves of the best.

Even if we do find happiness, we might feel guilty because there are other people who are less fortunate. The implicit, and false, assumption underlying such sentiments is that happiness is a zero-sum game—that one person's happiness (our own) necessarily deprives others of theirs. Williamson says, "As we let our light shine, we unconsciously give other people permission to do the same. As we are liberated from our own fear, our presence automatically liberates others." It is when we liberate ourselves from our fear of happiness that we can best help others.

## Inherent Worthiness

To lead a happy life, we must experience a sense of inherent worthiness. As Nathaniel Branden writes, "In order to seek values, man must consider himself worthy of enjoying them. In order to fight for his happiness, he must consider himself worthy of happiness." We must appreciate our core self, who we really are, independent of our tangible accomplishments; we must believe that we deserve to be happy; we must feel that we are worthy by virtue of our existence—because we are born with the heart and mind to experience pleasure and meaning.

When we do not accept our inherent worth, we ignore or actively undermine our talents, our potential, our joy, our accomplishments. For example, we might employ the "yes, but . . ." technique: "*Yes*, I do have meaning and pleasure in my life, *but* what if it doesn't last?" "*Yes*, I love my job, *but* what if I get bored, as I often do?" "*Yes*, I have found a partner I love, *but* what if she leaves me?" Refusing to accept the good things that happen to us leads to unhappiness and, given that we are still unhappy despite all the potential sources of happiness in our lives, to nihilism.

**TIME-IN** What, if any, internal and external factors are stopping you from becoming happier?

Before we are able to receive a gift, from a friend or from nature, we have to be open to it; a bottle with its cap screwed on tightly cannot be filled with water no matter how much water we try to pour into it or how often we try—the water simply runs down its sides, never filling it. Inherent worthiness is a state of openness—of being open to happiness.

## EXERCISE

### Sentence Completion

Here are some sentence stems that can help you overcome some of the possible barriers to happiness:

The things that stand in the way of my happiness . . .
To feel 5 percent more worthy of happiness . . .
If I refuse to live by other people's values . . .
If I succeed . . .
If I give myself the permission to be happy . . .
When I appreciate myself . . .
To bring 5 percent more happiness to my life . . .
I am beginning to see that . . .

Continue to do these and other sentence stems—from this book or from Branden's work—on a regular basis. The insights and behavioral changes that this simple exercise can generate are considerable.

13

# Fifth Meditation: Imagine

**Life would be infinitely happier if we could only be born at the age of eighty and gradually approach eighteen.**

—*Mark Twain*

You are one hundred and ten years old. A time machine has just been invented, and you are selected as one of the first people to use it. The inventor, a scientist from NASA, tells you that you will be transported back to the day when, as it happens, you first read *Happier.* You, with the wisdom of having lived and experienced life, have fifteen minutes to spend with your younger and less experienced self. What do you say when you meet? What advice do you give yourself?

I formulated this thought experiment after reading an account by psychiatrist Irvin Yalom of terminally ill cancer patients:

> An open confrontation with death allows many patients to move into a mode of existence that is richer than the one they experienced prior to their illness. Many patients report dramatic shifts in life perspective. They are able

> to trivialize the trivial, to assume a sense of control, to stop doing things they do not wish to do, to communicate more openly with families and close friends, and to live entirely in the present rather than in the future or the past. As one's focus turns from the trivial diversions of life, a fuller appreciation of the elemental factors in existence may emerge: the changing seasons, the falling leaves, the last spring, and especially, the loving of others. Over and over we hear our patients say, "Why did we have to wait until now, till we are riddled with cancer, to learn how to value and appreciate life?"

What struck me when I read accounts of terminally ill patients, whether by Yalom or others, is that following the news of their disease the patients were still the same people with the same knowledge of life's questions and answers, with the same cognitive and emotional capacities. No one descended from Mount Sinai presenting them with commandments on how to live; no Chinese, Indian, or Greek sage revealed to them the secrets to the good life; no one gave them mind- or heart-enhancing drugs; they did not discover a new and revolutionary self-help book that changed their lives.

Yet with the capacities they always had—which seemed to be inadequate in making them happy before—their lives changed. They gained no new knowledge but, rather, an acute awareness of what they knew all along. In other words, they had within them the knowledge of how they should live life. It was just that they ignored this knowledge or were not conscious of it.

What the time-travel thought experiment does is make us aware of life's brevity and preciousness. Granted, a hundred-and-ten-year-old has more experience—and there are no shortcuts in terms of gaining much of the wisdom that a full life can give us—but some of what we become aware of if we are lucky enough to live to be one hundred and ten we already know when we are fifty or even twenty. It is a matter of awareness. George Bernard Shaw's quip notwithstanding, youth does not need to be wasted on the young.[1]

**TIME-IN** Have you had experiences that made you reevaluate your priorities? Did you follow up on your new insights or understanding?

There is very little that any philosophy, psychology, or self-help book can teach us that is new about attaining the ultimate currency. The most a book or a teacher can do is to help raise our awareness, to help us become more fully in touch with what we already know. Ultimately, our progress, our growth, and our happiness come from our ability to look within ourselves and ask the important questions.

## EXERCISE

### Advice from Your Inner Sage

Do the exercise just described. Imagine that you are one hundred and ten years old or significantly older than you are now. Take fifteen minutes to give yourself advice on how to find more happiness in your life, starting at this point. Do the exercise in writing. As much as possible, ritualize the advice. If, for instance, your older self advises you to spend more time with your family, commit to an additional weekly or biweekly family outing.

Return to this exercise regularly—look at what you wrote, add to it, and ask yourself whether you have taken the advice of your inner sage.

14

# Sixth Meditation: Take Your Time

**The golden moments in the stream of life rush past us and we see nothing but sand; the angels come to visit us, and we only know them when they are gone.**

—*George Eliot*

Writing this book has been a deeply meaningful and pleasurable activity for me. There was, however, a period of a month or two during the summer of 2006 during which I did not look forward to writing, considered it as somewhat of a chore, and did not experience flow as often as I usually do. Why? Because something that I've come to see as one of the most important components of a happy life was missing: time.

That summer, I was putting the final touches on the manuscript, which I had promised my publishers by July 1, and at the same time was traveling around the country conducting workshops and giving lectures. While I was doing things that I love—teaching and writing both usually afford me pleasure and meaning—I had overcommitted myself. I compromised on my happiness because I had too much on my plate.

That so many of us are overcommitted may explain the surprising results of a study conducted by Daniel Kahneman and his colleagues. Women were asked to list and describe the activities in which they engaged the previous day and then report on how they felt during each activity. The women listed eating, working, taking care of their children, shopping, commuting, socializing, intimate relations, housework, and so on. The most unexpected finding was that, on aggregate, mothers did not particularly enjoy the time they spent taking care of their children.

Norbert Schwartz, one of Kahneman's coauthors on the article, explains the counterintuitive results of the study: "When people are asked how much they enjoy spending time with their kids they think of all the nice things—reading them a story or going to the zoo. But they don't take the other times into account, the times when they are trying to do something else and find the kids distracting." There is little doubt that most parents find child rearing meaningful—possibly the most meaningful experience in their lives—and yet as a result of having too much to do, the pleasure component of happiness is significantly reduced. Cell phones, e-mails, the information highway—the overall rising complexity of modern life—all contribute to the constant time pressure and to the experience of potentially enjoyable activities as distracting. "When there are too many competing demands on our time and attention, our ability to be present is diminished—and with it, our ability to appreciate and enjoy the experience."

Time pressure is pervasive and, to some extent, accounts for the culturewide increase in rates of depression. One of my roles as a tutor during my six years of graduate school was to help college students with their résumés. It astounded me that each year, students' accomplishments were more impressive than those of their predecessors, at least on paper. Initially, their awesome achievements impressed me—until I realized the emotional price they were paying for the smaller fonts and larger titles that were squeezed into the single page. In the same study that I mentioned at the beginning of this book, in which 45 percent of college students reported being depressed, 94 percent reported feeling "overwhelmed by everything they had to do."

We are, generally, too busy, trying to squeeze more and more activities into less and less time. Consequently, we fail to savor, to enjoy, potential sources of the ultimate currency that may be all around us—whether it is our work, a class, a piece of music, the landscape, our soul mate, or even our children.

**TIME-IN** In what areas or activities (if any) do you feel that you are compromising on your happiness because of time pressure?

What can we do, then, to enjoy our lives more despite the fast-paced rat-race environment so many of us live in? The answer to this question contains both bad news and good news. The bad news is that, unfortunately, there are no magic bullets—or magic pills. We must simplify our lives; we must slow down. The good news is that simplifying our lives, doing less rather than more, does not have to come at the expense of success.

## Simplify!

Henry David Thoreau admonished his contemporaries back in the nineteenth century to reduce the complexity in their daily lives: "Simplicity, simplicity, simplicity! I say let your affairs be as two or three, and not a hundred or a thousand; instead of a million count half a dozen." Thoreau's words are even more pertinent today, as our world becomes more complex and the pressure seems to mount by the nanosecond.

Time is a limited resource, and there are too many competing demands on this limited resource. Our immoderate busyness, the stress so many of us experience so much of the time, makes us unhappy across many areas of our lives. Researchers Susan and Clyde Hendrick point to the importance of simplifying for a healthy relationship: "If we can help people to simplify their lives, thus reducing their stress levels, it is very likely that people's relationships (including love and sex) would be enriched greatly. Moreover, the positive aspects of their lives would be enriched accordingly."

Psychologist Tim Kasser shows in his research that *time affluence* is a consistent predictor of well-being, whereas material affluence is not. Time affluence is the feeling that one has sufficient time to pursue activities that are personally meaningful, to reflect, to engage in leisure. Time poverty is the feeling that one is constantly stressed, rushed, overworked, behind. All we need to do is look around us—and often within ourselves—to realize the pervasiveness of time poverty in our culture.[1]

To raise our levels of well-being, there is no way around simplifying our lives. This means safeguarding our time, learning to say "no" more often—to people as well as opportunities—which is not easy. It means prioritizing, choosing activities that we really, really want to do, while letting go of others. Fortunately, though, doing less does not necessarily entail compromising on our success.

## When Less Is More

One of the main themes of this book is that it is possible to be both successful and happy; time and again, I've challenged the "no pain, no gain" maxim. While some pain is necessary for growth—be it of a muscle or of character—the notion that we cannot grow and prosper while enjoying our lives is blatantly false. Research on flow, for example, illustrates that peak experience (enjoying ourselves) and peak performance (doing our best) go hand in hand. To increase the likelihood of flow, we need to engage in activities that are neither too easy nor too difficult. The same general principle applies to our management of time.

In her *Harvard Business Review* article "Creativity Under the Gun," Teresa Amabile dispels the myth that working under pressure yields better results: "When creativity is under the gun, it usually ends up getting killed. Although time pressure may drive people to work more and get more done, and may even make them *feel* more creative, it actually causes them, in general, to think less creatively." While working hard is certainly necessary for success, working too hard will probably hurt, not help, that success.

Time pressure leads to frustration, and when we're frustrated or experience other negative emotions, our thinking becomes more constricted, narrower, and less broad and creative. Moreover, Amabile found that people are unaware of this phenomenon and live under the illusion that when they are experiencing time pressure they are also more creative. This explains why it is so difficult to get out of the pressure cooker, the rat race: the perception of creativity leads to the perpetuation of the stress.

Amabile's study revealed the phenomenon of "pressure hangover"—in which high levels of pressure decreased creativity not only for the period in which the person felt pressured, but for up to days later.[2] When we try to do too much, we compromise our potential for growth, both in terms of the ultimate currency as well as in terms of our quantifiable success. As J. P. Morgan, one of the most successful and creative entrepreneurs of all time, said, "I can do a year's work in nine months, but not in twelve." Sometimes, indeed, less is more.

Even if the individual activities in which we engage have the potential to make us happy, we can still be unhappy on aggregate.

Just as the most delicious food in the world—be it chocolate, lasagna, or a hamburger—cannot be enjoyed if consumed in too large quantities, neither can we enjoy activities, no matter how potentially "delicious" they are, if we have too much of them. Quantity affects quality; there *can* be too much of a good thing.

A wine connoisseur does not chug the entire glass of wine in one gulp; to fully enjoy the richness of the drink, she smells, she tastes, she savors, she takes her time. To become a life connoisseur, to enjoy the richness that life has to offer, we, too, need to take our time.

## EXERCISE

### Simplify!

Go back to the "Mapping Your Life" exercise at the end of Chapter 3. If you have not yet completed it or did it a while back, write down the activities you were engaged in over the last week or two. Looking at the list or your life map, answer the following questions: Where can I simplify? What can I give up? Am I spending too much time on the Internet or watching TV? Can I reduce the number of meetings at work or the duration of some of the meetings? Am I saying "yes" to activities to which I can say "no"?

Commit to reducing the busyness in your life. In addition, ritualize times when you can dedicate yourself fully, with undivided attention, to things you find both meaningful and pleasurable: spending time with your family, gardening, focusing on a project at work, meditating, watching a film, and so on.

15

# Seventh Meditation: The Happiness Revolution

**The world has to learn that the actual pleasure derived from material things is of rather low quality on the whole and less even in quantity than it looks to those who have not tried it.**

—*Oliver Wendell Holmes*

The benefits of the scientific revolution are too many to count. In agriculture, farmers turned away from praying to the rain god and instead invested their energies in cultivating the soil; we now have the capacity, though it remains unrealized, to feed every person on Earth. In medicine, the shift was from the witch doctor's brew to penicillin; life expectancy rose from approximately twenty-five years during the Middle Ages to almost seventy today.[1] In astronomy, a flat Earth mounted on turtles gave way to a round Earth revolving around the sun; we have landed a man on the moon and are constantly expanding our frontiers.

Given such impressive results, most people naturally have faith in science; it has become the religion of modernity. But science, in and of itself, is not the answer to all of our problems, personal or societal, and in fact our perception of science as omnipotent can lead to a new set of challenges. One of these challenges, a by-product of the scientific revolution, is the prevalence of *material perception*, the belief that the material is the highest on the hierarchy of importance.

Throughout much of the world, the scientific revolution rejected the mystical—belief in rain gods, witch doctors, or giant turtles—but along with the mystical, anything nonmaterial and unquantifiable was discarded, too. The proverbial baby was thrown out with the bathwater. Happiness and spirituality—which are closely linked[2]—were discarded as immaterial, losing their value in our post–scientific revolution world. Material perception accounts, at least in part, for the obsession with material wealth and the ensuing unhappiness.

Lest I be misunderstood, my criticism of material perception is not, in any way, a criticism of the capitalist system, which has freedom at its core. Winston Churchill once commented that "the inherent vice of capitalism is the unequal sharing of blessings; the inherent virtue of socialism is the equal sharing of miseries." History as well as research in social science have proven Churchill correct—people are generally happier in free countries than they are under state-controlled economies. The problem arises when the freedom to pursue material wealth is replaced with a compulsion to amass it.

The alternative to material perception is *happiness perception*, which is about moving away from seeing the material as the highest end, as our central pursuit.

## Happiness Perception

Happiness perception is about recognizing that happiness is the ultimate currency, the end toward which all other goals lead. Happiness perception is *not* about rejecting the material but rather dethroning it from its status as the highest on the hierarchy. Aristotle understood this when he wrote that "happiness is the meaning and the purpose of life, the whole aim and end of human existence," as did the Dalai Lama, who asserted that "whether one believes in religion or not, whether one believes in this religion or that religion, the very purpose of our life is happiness, the very motion of our life is towards happiness." The currency through which we take stock of our life—our perception of what matters—has wide-reaching consequences, for our personal lives and for society as a whole. We enjoy higher levels of well-being when we recognize and internalize the fact that happiness is the ultimate currency.

When the questions that guide our life are about finding more meaning and pleasure (happiness perception) rather than about how we can acquire more money and more possessions (material perception), we are much more likely to derive benefit from the journey as well as the destination. Today, with the prevalence of material perception, too many people are asking the wrong questions. Students mostly wonder how college can help them make more money; when choosing work, they have questions primarily about prestige and progress. No wonder levels of depression are on the rise.

Happiness perception is about asking the question of questions, "What will make me happier?" It is about finding the overlap among the three questions "What gives me meaning?" "What gives me pleasure?" "What are my strengths?" It is about asking, "What is my calling?" and identifying the things that you really,

really want to do at school, at work, and with your life as a whole. With these questions comes a much higher likelihood that you will find the ultimate currency.

## A Peaceful Revolution

I believe that the spread of happiness perception can bring about a society-wide revolution, no less significant than what Karl Marx had hoped to achieve. The Marxist revolution ultimately failed, though not before claiming millions of lives and making many more miserable. Because the means it used were immoral from the outset—taking away freedom from the individual—it was doomed to bring little more than destruction and unhappiness. The happiness revolution, when it comes about, will lead to radically different outcomes, through radically different means.

In contrast to Marx's proposed revolution, which was going to be externally driven, the happiness revolution must come from within. Marx was a materialist; he believed that history was driven by material conditions and therefore that change had to come from the outside, through material means. The happiness revolution, which is about the change from material perception to happiness perception, is mental and therefore internal. No outside force is required to bring about this change; no such force is capable of bringing about this change. Conscious choice—the choice to focus on happiness as the ultimate currency—is the only change agent.

A happiness revolution will come about when people recognize, in theory and in practice, that happiness is the ultimate currency. While many people would agree, in theory, that this is true, a closer look at the way they lead their lives reveals that in effect they are driven primarily by factors other than happiness. Happiness perception can help us, as a society, emerge from the "great depression" in which we currently find ourselves. The implications to society, though, go beyond raising our collective levels of well-being.

What would happen if most people internalized the change from material to happiness perception? First, envy, among individuals and cultures, would be reduced considerably. In a leadership seminar that I once conducted, some participants drew an analogy between people in an organization and crabs about to be boiled in a pot. When a crab attempts to get out of the pot, the other crabs pull it back in—not because pulling it down will help them get out but because they do not want the other crab to get out while they boil. The need to bring others down comes from a materialistic perception of a world in which resources are a zero-sum game and one's success implies another's failure, where one's gain is another's loss.

More generally, if happiness perception prevails, individual and international conflicts would be reduced significantly. Most wars are fought over land, oil, gold, and other material goods. The leaders in these countries who are responsible for fueling these conflicts accept the false premise that the ultimate currency for their country—and for themselves—is how much material wealth they possess.

Accepting this premise leads countries and individuals to conflict because some material resources are finite. But a win-win solution to most conflicts can be found once people on both sides realize the true nature of the ultimate currency. Given that happiness depends more on internal rather than external circumstances, there should be no conflict of interest when it comes to spreading the ultimate currency. The quantity of happiness is not fixed: an abundance of happiness for one person or country does not deprive another. The pursuit of happiness does not set up a zero-sum game but a positive-sum game—everyone can be better off. As the Buddha said, "Thousands of candles can be lighted from a single candle, and the life of the candle will not be shortened. Happiness never decreases by being shared." Unlike material possessions, which are usually finite, happiness is infinite.[3]

My hope that we might be able to reframe interpersonal or international conflicts is not a call for pacifism; focusing on the short-term benefits of appeasement while ignoring the long-term consequences will lead neither to peace nor to happiness.[4] A person or a country that is attacked should not invite the enemy to the negotiating table to explain that happiness is actually the ultimate currency. In international as well as interpersonal relations, it usually takes two to dance the happiness tango.

**TIME-IN** How will your life change if you shift, in theory and in practice, further toward happiness perception?

The happiness revolution will not come about through confiscating wealth and redistributing it to the masses but rather through an internal revolution in perception. It will not come about through a bloody revolt that rids society of millions of potential dissenters but rather through a conceptual revolt that will shed the shackles of materialism that compromise our potential for the ultimate currency.

The happiness revolution is about creating a society-wide paradigm shift to a higher level of consciousness, a higher plane of existence—to happiness perception. If most people in our society understand and internalize the ideas that happiness is not a zero-sum game and that pursuing it does not put us in competition with others, a quiet revolution will unfold where the pursuit of happiness and helping others attain higher levels of happiness will be two complementary ends. When this revolution comes about, we will witness a society-wide abundance of not only happiness but also goodness.

## EXERCISE

### Conflict Resolution

Think of a conflict, major or minor, that you have with another person or a group. In writing, elaborate on the price that you and the other party are paying in the ultimate currency. Is the price worth it? If not, elaborate on possible solutions that could maximize happiness for you as well as for the other person or group.

For example, is it worth your while to hold a grudge against someone who was a friend and let you down once? Is it making you, and her, happier? Should you maybe raise the topic with her and, after acknowledging that you were hurt, do what you can to resume the friendship, which was, and could possibly still be, a source of happiness?

Experiencing negative emotions toward others may be justified, and having them is often natural, even healthy. A state of conflict is at times unavoidable, and trying to wage peace at all cost could lead to more unhappiness in the long run. Nevertheless, for one reason or another, many people unnecessarily hold on to anger or resentment toward family members, former friends, or entire groups—when instead they could forgive, let go, and move on.

Whether we decide to forgive and reconcile or to condemn and disengage, the key is to use happiness as the standard for evaluation. To do so, we need to ask ourselves the simple question with the complex answer: which path will lead to the highest profits in the ultimate currency?

Conclusion

# Here and Now

**Be the change you want to see in the world.**

—*Gandhi*

I am optimistic about the possibility of change toward a more emotionally prosperous society. I believe that people *can* find work that will provide them present and future benefit, that people *can* find education a rich source of the ultimate currency, that people *can* find meaningful and pleasurable relationships. I believe that the happiness revolution will come about. I do not, however, believe that these changes will happen overnight.

In this book I present a neat and structured theory of happiness, but life is neither neat nor structured. A theory, at best, can establish a stable Archimedean point amid the flux of life, a platform from which we can ask the right questions. Of course, making the transition from theory to practice is difficult: changing deeply rooted habits of thinking, transforming ourselves and our world, requires a great deal of effort.

People often abandon theories when they discover how difficult it is to put them into practice. It seems odd that most of us are prepared to work extremely hard for quantifiable ends yet give up quickly when it comes to pursuing the ultimate currency. If we want to find happiness, we must commit ourselves to working hard at it, for while there is one easy step to *un*happiness—doing nothing—there are no easy steps to happiness.

## If Not Now, When

My friend Kim and I walked around Provincetown, admiring the quaint shops on the main street, listening to the waves breaking on the rocks, breathing in the salty air, savoring that precious feeling of being outside of time that can come when one is in a small town on vacation.

At the time, I was a graduate student living in the competitive environment of the university. I told Kim that as soon as I graduated, I wanted to move to a place like Provincetown. I thought that without the looming deadlines and the deadly pace, I would finally experience the calm I had been looking for my entire life. I had often thought about moving to a quiet place after graduation, but as the idea took on the form of words—became tangible—I felt uneasy.

Had I not just fallen into the trap of living in the future? Did I really have to wait until graduation? Kim and I had been working on this book together and were talking and thinking a lot about the question of happiness. We had been talking about how, despite being in a competitive environment, with a great deal of work, and keeping a fast pace, we could still experience calm. Kim said, "The calmness has to be inside. If you're happy, that happiness is transportable—you take it with you wherever you go." She paused and then added, "Not that the external isn't significant, but it doesn't *make* us happy."

We often imagine that when we reach some future destination, we will feel accomplished, calm, and ready for happiness. We tell ourselves that, with the attainment of certain goals, we will finally find peace. We tell ourselves that this will happen once we graduate from college, or get tenure, or make enough money, or have a family and children, or—reach any other number of goals that will likely change over the course of our lives. Yet in most cases, shortly after reaching some destination, we return to our base level of well-being. If we are normally anxious and stressed, those feelings will likely return soon after reaching a goal we thought would change our lives.

Much of the rat racer's tension stems from the need to feel control over the future. As a result, she lives in the future. The rat racer lives by the "what *if*" rather than by the "what *is*"—in the tense hypothetical future rather than in the calm real present. What if I don't do well on the exam? What if I don't get a promotion? What if I can't afford the mortgage on my new house? Rather than fully experiencing the here and now, she is, in the words of poet Galway Kinnell, "smearing the darkness of expectation across experience."

Then there are those who, stuck in the past, do not allow themselves to experience happiness in the present. They rehearse their unsatisfying histories, their attempts to live first as rat racers and then as hedonists; they brood over the relationships they tried to rekindle to no avail, the many jobs they worked at without finding their true calling. Always reliving the past, concerned with justifying their unhappiness, they forgo the potential for happiness in their lives. Rather than allowing ourselves to remain enslaved by our past or future, we must learn to make the most of what is presently in front of us and all around us.

## This Is It

One of the common barriers to happiness is the false expectation that one thing—a book or a teacher, a princess or a knight, an accomplishment, a prize, or a revelation—will bring us eternal bliss. While all these things can contribute to our well-being, at best they form a small part of the mosaic of a happy life. The fairy-tale notion of happiness—the belief that something would carry us to the happily ever after—inevitably leads to disappointment. A happy—or happier—life is rarely shaped by some extraordinary life-changing event; rather, it is shaped incrementally, experience by experience, moment by moment.

To realize, to make real, life's potential for the ultimate currency, we must first accept that "this is it"—that *all* there is to life is the day-to-day, the ordinary, the details of the mosaic. We are living a happy life when we derive pleasure and meaning while spending time with our loved ones, or learning something new, or engaging in a project at work. The more our days are filled with these experiences, the happier we become. *This is all there is to it.*

# Notes

## Preface

1. This definition is taken from *The Positive Psychology Manifesto*, which was first introduced by some of the leading researchers in the field in 1999. The full definition: "Positive Psychology is the scientific study of optimal human functioning. It aims to discover and promote the factors that allow individuals and communities to thrive. The positive psychology movement represents a new commitment on the part of research psychologists to focus attention upon the sources of psychological health, thereby going beyond prior emphases upon disease and disorder." The full manifesto can be found online: http://www.ppc.sas.upenn.edu/akumalmanifesto.htm.

## Chapter 1

1. Research by Daniel Goleman, Richard Boyatzis, and Annie McKee shows how most change efforts fail after "the honeymoon phase"—after the initial implementation stage. See also Kotter, J. P. (1996). *Leading Change.* Harvard Business School Press.
2. When I was playing squash and training for six hours a day, people would often comment on my "discipline," which never made sense to me. While I put in a great deal of effort on the court or in the gym, getting to the court or to the gym was effortless—it was an automatic ritual that I carried out daily.

3. According to William James, it takes twenty-one days to form a new habit. Loehr and Schwartz (2004) believe that most activities become a habit in less than a month. They quote the Dalai Lama, who said, "There isn't anything that isn't made easier through constant familiarity and training. Through training we can change; we can transform ourselves."

## Chapter 2

1. Based on Pennebaker, J. W. (1997). *Opening Up*. The Guilford Press; and Burton, C. M., and King, L. A. (2004). The Health Benefits of Writing About Intensely Positive Experiences. *Journal of Research in Personality*, 38, 150–163. In addition to Pennebaker's work in *Opening Up*, other books that can help you think about journaling are Ira Progoff's *At a Journal Workshop* and Karen Horney's *Self Analysis*.
2. These are the ABCs of psychology: *A*ffect (your emotions), *B*ehaviors (what you did), and *C*ognition (your thoughts). To enjoy lasting change, it is best to combine all three.

## Chapter 3

1. In *Authentic Happiness*, Martin Seligman identifies three components of happiness: meaning, pleasure, and engagement.
2. In the Third Meditation, I elaborate on the distinction between emotional highs or lows and a deep sense of happiness.
3. I further discuss the importance of challenge in Chapter 6.
4. Another way of characterizing happiness is that it comprises both a cognitive, evaluative component (the meaning we attribute to an experience) and an emotional, affective component (the experience of pleasure).

5. In research on positive affect and meaning in life, Laura King and her colleagues show that "positive moods may predispose individuals to feel that life is meaningful." King, L. A., Hicks, J. A., Krull, J., and Del Gaiso, A. K. (2006). Positive Affect and the Experience of Meaning in Life. *Journal of Personality and Social Psychology*, 90, 179–196.
6. Nathaniel Branden discusses the importance of integrity for our self-esteem and happiness. Branden, N. (1994). *The Six Pillars of Self-Esteem*. Bantam Books.
7. Research by Chris Argyris shows that we are generally good at identifying discrepancies between what others say is important to them (their "espoused theories") and what they actually do (their "theories-in-use") but not so effective identifying similar discrepancies in our lives. Therefore, it may be useful to do this exercise with someone who knows you well and cares about you enough to be willing to help you evaluate your life. According to Argyris (1976), "Espoused theories of action are those that people report as a basis for actions. Theories-in-use are the theories of action inferred from how people actually behave."
8. Research commissioned by Hewlett-Packard and conducted by TNS Research illustrates that "workers distracted by phone calls, e-mails, and text messages suffer a greater loss of IQ than a person smoking marijuana." See story on CNN .com, retrieved on November 21, 2006: http://edition.cnn.com/2005/WORLD/europe/04/22/text.iq.

## Chapter 4

1. For an explanation of the technique, see Branden, N. (1994). *The Six Pillars of Self-Esteem*. Bantam Books; as well as nathaniel branden.com/catalog/articles_essays/instructions.html.

2. I highly recommend doing a longer sentence-completion program, such as the one found in Nathaniel Branden's *Six Pillars of Self-Esteem* or online. For example, see nathanielbranden.com/catalog/articles_essays/sentence_completion.html.

## Chapter 5

1. For a good overview of the academic literature, see Locke, E. A., and Latham, G. P. (2002). Building a Practically Useful Theory of Goal Setting and Task Motivation: A 35-Year Odyssey. *American Psychologist*, 57(9), 705–717.
2. See Rosenthal, R., and Jacobson, L. (1968). *Pygmalion in the Classroom: Teacher Expectation and Pupils' Intellectual Development*. Holt, Reinhardt and Winston; and Bandura, A. (1997). *Self-Efficacy: The Exercise of Control*. W. H. Freeman and Company.
3. Philip Stone introduced me to the idea of being while doing.
4. In his book *Happiness*, Matthieu Ricard points out the problem with the expression "killing time." Ricard, M. (2006). *Happiness: A Guide to Developing Life's Most Important Skill*. Little, Brown and Company.
5. For a more elaborate process, see Chapter 11 of *Built to Last*. Collins, J., and Porras, J. I. (2002). *Built to Last: Successful Habits of Visionary Companies*. HarperCollins.
6. Research in the area of cognitive dissonance (Festinger, L. [1957]. *A Theory of Cognitive Dissonance*. Stanford University Press) and self-perception theory (Bem, D. J. [1967]. Self-Perception: An Alternative Interpretation of Cognitive Dissonance Phenomena. *Psychological Review*, 74, 183–200) suggests that when we endorse a certain position, our commitment to the position is strengthened. So if we tell others how important the ultimate currency is and remind them to

pursue meaningful and pleasurable activities, we are making it more likely that we ourselves pursue activities that will make us happier.

## Chapter 6

1. I am not advocating a laissez-faire approach to education in which parents simply cater to their children's whims, allowing them to indulge their immediate likes or dislikes. The most successful educators find a balance between externally imposed boundaries and democratic practices, between firmness and allowing for independence. For a more in-depth discussion of child rearing and educational practices, see Lillard, P. P. (1996). *Montessori Today: A Comprehensive Approach to Education from Birth to Adulthood*. Schocken Books; and Ginott, H. G. (1995). *Teacher and Child: A Book for Parents and Teachers*. Collier Books.
2. Csikszentmihalyi's work on flow has wide implications for the individual and for society. For a more complete discussion, see Csikszentmihalyi, M. (1998). *Finding Flow: The Psychology of Engagement with Everyday Life*. Basic Books.
3. I will elaborate on this and other related ideas in much greater depth in my forthcoming book *The Permission to Be Human*.

## Chapter 7

1. Survey conducted by the Conference Board (2005). See online report: conference-board.org/utilities/pressDetail.cfm?press_ID=2582.
2. See Wrzesniewski, A., and Dutton, J. E. (2001). Crafting a Job: Revisioning Employees as Active Crafters of Their Work. *Academy of Management Journal*, 26, 179–201. Originally, the distinction between a job, a career, and a calling was made in

the book *Habits of the Heart*. Bellah, R. N., Madsen, R., Sullivan, W. M., Swidler, A., and Tipton, S. M. (1996). *Habits of the Heart: Individualism and Commitment in American Life*. University of California Press.

3. For a more elaborate discussion of identifying personal strengths, see Buckingham M., and Clifton, D. O. (2001). *Now, Discover Your Strengths*. Free Press.
4. The same applies to how we craft other aspects of our lives. For example, if we identify and highlight the positive elements of our relationships, we are more likely to be happy in them.

## Chapter 8

1. See Bem, D. J. (1996). Exotic Becomes Erotic: A Developmental Theory of Sexual Orientation. *Psychological Review*, 103, 320–335.
2. John Gottman elaborates on the idea of "love maps." Gottman, J. M. (2000). *The Seven Principles for Making Marriage Work: A Practical Guide from the Country's Foremost Relationship Expert*. Three Rivers Press.

## Chapter 9

1. See Hoffman, M. L. (1991). Empathy, Social Cognition, and Moral Action. In *Handbook of Moral Behavior and Development*. Edited by W. M. Kurtines and J. L. Gewirtz. Lawrence Erlbaum Associates, Inc.; Smith, A. (1976). *The Theory of Moral Sentiments*. Oxford University Press; and Wilson, J. Q. (1993). *The Moral Sense*. Free Press.

## Chapter 10

1. I discuss this research on self-concordant goals in more depth in Chapter 5.

## Chapter 11

1. Lecture at the Gallup International Positive Psychology Summit, October 7, 2006.
2. To learn more about this powerful intervention, see http://appreciativeinquiry.case.edu.

## Chapter 13

1. George Bernard Shaw, the Irish playwright, critic, and Nobel Prize winner in literature, remarked that "youth is wasted on the young."

## Chapter 14

1. Discussed in Peterson, C. (2006). *A Primer in Positive Psychology*. Oxford University Press. Leslie Perlow addresses a similar idea, the notion of "time famine," in the context of the workplace. Perlow, L. (1999). The Time Famine: Towards a Sociology of Work Time. *Administrative Science Quarterly*, 44, 57–81.
2. Amabile found one exception to the rule: pressure actually yielded creativity when the person worked on a single project, felt a sense of urgency and a sense of mission, and was able to devote undivided attention to that project. This explains the success of the Apollo 13 mission, for example. Unfortunately, in today's workplace, time pressure often goes hand in hand with feeling like there is too much on one's plate—and the lack of focus leads to poor performance. It is rare in modern organizations, Amabile shows, to be able to immerse oneself undisturbed in an important and urgent problem.

## Chapter 15

1. Data reported on the website of the Foundation for Teaching Economics: fte.org/capitalism/introduction/02.php.

2. Research links spirituality with happiness. See, for example, Emmons, R. A., and McCullough, M. E. (2004). *The Psychology of Gratitude.* Oxford University Press. Spirituality is often associated with religion, but it does not have to be. In Chapter 3 I highlighted the link between spirituality and significance; a person who finds her activities significant, or meaningful, is more likely to experience spirituality and, hence, happiness.
3. While I do not agree that material wealth is a zero-sum game—capitalism has shown that the size of the pie is not fixed (that is, that wealth can be created)—material perception is about seeing the material as finite and, hence, as part of a zero-sum game.
4. Pacifism, though usually well-intentioned, has led to great losses, both in lives as well as in the ultimate currency. As Winston Churchill said, "Acts of appeasement today will have to be remedied at far greater cost and remorse tomorrow."

# References

Amabile, T. M., Hadley, C. N., and Kramer, S. J. (2002). Creativity Under the Gun. *Harvard Business Review*, August 1.

Argyris, C. (1976). Single-Loop and Double-Loop Models in Research on Decision Making. *Administrative Science Quarterly*, 21, 363–375.

Badaracco, J. L. (1997). *Defining Moments*. Harvard Business School Press.

Bandura, A. (1997). *Self-Efficacy: The Exercise of Control*. W. H. Freeman and Company.

Bellah, R. N., Madsen, R., Sullivan, W. M., Swidler, A., and Tipton, S. M. (1996). *Habits of the Heart: Individualism and Commitment in American Life*. University of California Press.

Bem, D. J. (1996). Exotic Becomes Erotic: A Developmental Theory of Sexual Orientation. *Psychological Review*, 103, 320–335.

Bem, D. J. (1967). Self-Perception: An Alternative Interpretation of Cognitive Dissonance Phenomena. *Psychological Review*, 74, 183–200.

Benson, H. (2000). *The Relaxation Response*. Harper.

Bexton, W. H., Heron, W., and Scott, T. H. (1954). Effects of Decreased Variation in the Sensory Environment. *Canadian Journal of Psychology*, 8, 70–76.

Boldt, L. G. (1999). *Zen and the Art of Making a Living: A Practical Guide to Creative Career Design*. Penguin.

Branden, N. (1985). *The Psychology of Romantic Love.* Bantam.

Branden, N. (1994). *The Six Pillars of Self-Esteem.* Bantam Books.

Branden, N. In Ayn Rand (1989). *The Virtue of Selfishness.* New American Library.

Brickman, P., Coates, D., and Bulman, R. J. (1978). Lottery Winners and Accident Victims: Is Happiness Relative? *Journal of Personality and Social Psychology*, 36, 917–927.

Bronner, E. (1998). College Freshmen Aiming for High Marks in Income. *New York Times*, January 12.

Buckingham, M., and Clifton, D. O. (2001). *Now, Discover Your Strengths.* Free Press.

Burton, C. M., and King, L. A. (2004). The Health Benefits of Writing About Intensely Positive Experiences. *Journal of Research in Personality*, 38, 150–163.

Campbell, J., and Moyers, B. (1991). *The Power of Myth.* Anchor.

Collins, J., and Porras, J. I. (2002). *Built to Last: Successful Habits of Visionary Companies.* HarperCollins.

Collins, M. (1992). *Ordinary Children, Extraordinary Teachers.* Hampton Roads.

Coopersmith, S. (1967). *The Antecedents of Self-Esteem.* Freeman.

Covey, S. R. (2004). *The Seven Habits of Highly Effective People.* Free Press.

Csikszentmihalyi, M. (1998). *Finding Flow: The Psychology of Engagement with Everyday Life.* Basic Books.

Csikszentmihalyi, M. (1990). *Flow: The Psychology of Optimal Experience.* Harper and Row.

Csikszentmihalyi, M., and Lefevre, J. (1989). Optimal Experience in Work and Leisure. *Journal of Personality and Social Psychology*, 56, 815–822.

Damasio, A. R. (1995). *Descartes' Error: Emotion, Reason and the Human Brain.* Avon Books.

Davidson, J. R., Kabat-Zinn, J., Schumacher, J., Rosenkranz, M., Muller, D., Santorelli, S. F., Urbanowski, F., Harrington, A., Bonus, K., and Sheridan, J. F. (2003). Alterations in Brain and Immune Function Produced by Mindfulness Meditation. *Psychosomatic Medicine*, 65, 564–570.

Diener, E., and Seligman, M. E. P. (2002). Very Happy People. *Psychological Science*, 13, 80–83.

Diener, E., and Suh, E. M. (2003). *Culture and Subjective Well-Being*. The MIT Press.

Diener, E., Suh, E. M., Lucas, R. E., and Smith, H. L. (1999). Subjective Well-Being: Three Decades of Progress. *Psychological Bulletin*, 125, 276–302.

Emmons, R. A. (1999). Religion in the Psychology of Personality. *Journal of Personality*, 67, 873–888.

Emmons, R. A., and McCullough, M. E. (2004). *The Psychology of Gratitude*. Oxford University Press.

Festinger, L. (1957). *A Theory of Cognitive Dissonance*. Stanford University Press.

Foster, D. J., and Wilson, M. A. (2006). Reverse Replay of Behavioural Sequences in Hippocampal Place Cells During the Awake State. *Nature*, 440, 680–683.

Frankl, V. E. (2006). *Man's Search for Meaning*. Beacon Press.

Fredrickson, B. L. (1998). What Good Are Positive Emotions? *Review of General Psychology*, 2, 300–319.

Gardner, J. (1990). *On Leadership*. Free Press.

George, J. M. (1991). State or Trait: Effects of Positive Mood on Prosocial Behaviors at Work. *Journal of Applied Psychology*, 76, 299–307.

Gilbert, D. T. (2006). *Stumbling on Happiness*. Knopf.

Gilbert, D. T., Pinel, E. C., Wilson, T. D., Blumberg, S. J., and Wheatley, T. P. (1998). Immune Neglect: A Source of Durability Bias in Affective Forecasting. *Journal of Personality and Social Psychology*, 75, 617–638.

Ginott, H. G. (1995). *Teacher and Child: A Book for Parents and Teachers.* Collier Books.

Goldberg, C. (2006). Is Instant Replay a Learning Tool? *Boston Globe*, February 20.

Goleman, D. (1995). *Emotional Intelligence.* Bantam Books.

Goleman, D., Boyatzis, R., and McKee, A. (2004). *Primal Leadership: Learning to Lead with Emotional Intelligence.* Harvard Business Press.

Gottman, J. M. (2000). *The Seven Principles for Making Marriage Work: A Practical Guide from the Country's Foremost Relationship Expert.* Three Rivers Press.

Hackman, J. R., and Oldham, G. R. (1976). Motivation Through the Design of Work: Test of a Theory. *Organizational Behavior and Human Performance*, 16, 250–279.

Hatfield, E., Traupmann, J., Sprecher, S., Utne, M., and Hay, J. (1985). Equity and Intimate Relations: Recent Research. In W. Ickes (ed.), *Compatible and Incompatible Relationships.* Springer-Verlag.

Hebb, D. O. (1955). Drives and the C.N.S. (Conceptual Nervous System). *Psychological Review*, 62, 243–254.

Hendrick, S., and Hendrick, C. (2002). Love. In C. R. Snyder and S. J. Lopez (eds.), *Handbook of Positive Psychology*, 472–484. Oxford University Press.

Hoffman, M. L. (1991). Empathy, Social Cognition, and Moral Action. In W. M. Kurtines and J. L. Gewirtz (eds.), *Handbook of Moral Behavior and Development.* Lawrence Erlbaum Associates, Inc.

Isen, A. M., Clark, M., and Schwartz, M. F. (1976). Duration of the Effect of Good Mood on Helping: Footprints on the Sands of Time. *Journal of Personality and Social Psychology*, 34, 385–393.

James, W. (1907). *Pragmatism, a New Name for Some Old Ways of Thinking: Popular Lectures on Philosophy.* Longmans, Green, and Company.

Jung, C. G. (1955). *Modern Man in Search of a Soul.* Harvest.

Kabat-Zinn, J. (1990). *Full Catastrophe Living: The Wisdom of Your Body and Mind to Face Stress, Pain, and Illness.* Delta.

Kadison, R. (2005). Getting an Edge—Use of Stimulants and Anti-Depressants in College. *New England Journal of Medicine*, 1089–1091.

Kahneman, D., Krueger, A. B., Schkade, D., Schwartz, N., and Stone, A. A. (2006). Would You Be Happier if You Were Richer? A Focusing Illusion. *Science*, 312, 1908–1910.

Kant, I. (1985). *Foundations of the Metaphysics of Morals.* Translated by L. W. Beck. Macmillan Publishing Company.

Kasser, T., and Ahuvia, A. (2002). Materialistic Values and Well-Being in Business Students. *European Journal of Social Psychology*, 32, 137–146.

King, L. A., Hicks, J. A., Krull, J., and Del Gaiso, A. K. (2006). Positive Affect and the Experience of Meaning in Life. *Journal of Personality and Social Psychology*, 90, 179–196.

Kotter, J. P. (1996). *Leading Change.* Harvard Business School Press.

Langer, E. (1989). *Mindfulness.* Addison-Wesley.

Layard, R. (2006). *Happiness: Lessons from a New Science.* Penguin.

Lillard, P. P. (1996). *Montessori Today: A Comprehensive Approach to Education from Birth to Adulthood.* Schocken Books.

Locke, E. A., and Latham, G. P. (2002). Building a Practically Useful Theory of Goal Setting and Task Motivation: A 35-Year Odyssey. *American Psychologist*, 57(9), 705–717.

Loehr, J., and Schwartz, T. (2004). *The Power of Full Engagement: Managing Energy, Not Time, Is the Key to High Performance and Personal Time.* Free Press.

Lykken, D., and Tellegen, A. (1996). Happiness Is a Stochastic Phenomenon. *Psychological Science*, 7, 186–189.

Lyubomirsky, S., Sheldon, K. M., and Schkade, D. (2005). Pursuing Happiness: The Architecture of Sustainable Change. *Review of General Psychology*, 9, 111–131.

Maltz, M. (1960). *Psycho-Cybernetics.* Pocket Books.

Maslow, A. H. (1993). *The Farther Reaches of Human Nature.* Penguin.

McCullough, M. E., and Witvliet, C. V. (2002). The Psychology of Forgiveness. In C. R. Snyder and S. J. Lopez (eds.), *Handbook of Positive Psychology*, 446–458. Oxford University Press.

Murray, W. H. (1951). *The Scottish Himalayan Expedition.* J. M. Dent and Sons.

Myers, D. G. (2000). The Funds, Friends, and Faith of Happy People. *American Psychologist*, 55, 56–67.

Neyfakh, L. (2006). The Science of Smiling. *The Harvard Crimson.*

Nozick, R. (1977). *Anarchy, State and Utopia.* Basic Books.

Palmer, P. (1997). *The Courage to Teach: Exploring the Inner Landscape of a Teacher's Life.* Jossey-Bass.

Pennebaker, J. W. (1997). *Opening Up.* The Guilford Press.

Perlow, L. (1999). The Time Famine: Towards a Sociology of Work Time. *Administrative Science Quarterly*, 44, 57–81.

Peterson, C. (2006). *A Primer in Positive Psychology.* Oxford University Press.

Peterson, P., Maier, S. F., and Seligman, M. E. P. (1995). *Learned Helplessness: A Theory for the Age of Personal Control.* Oxford University Press.

Pirsig, R. M. (1984). *Zen and the Art of Motorcycle Maintenance: An Inquiry into Values.* Bantam Books.

Ricard, M. (2006). *Happiness: A Guide to Developing Life's Most Important Skill.* Little, Brown and Company.

Rosenthal, R., and Jacobson, L. (1968). *Pygmalion in the Classroom: Teacher Expectation and Pupils' Intellectual Development.* Holt, Reinhardt and Winston.

Russel, B. (1930). *The Conquest of Happiness.* Horace Liveright.

Schnarch, D. (1998). *Passionate Marriage: Keeping Love and Intimacy Alive in Committed Relationships.* Owl Books.

Seligman, M. E. P. (2004). *Authentic Happiness: Using the New Positive Psychology to Realize Your Potential for Lasting Fulfillment.* Free Press.

Seligman, M. E. P. (1990). *Learned Optimism: How to Change Your Mind and Your Life.* Pocket Books.

Sheldon, K. M., and Elliot, A. J. (1999). Goal Striving, Need Satisfaction, and Longitudinal Well-Being: The Self-Concordance Model. *Journal of Personality and Social Psychology*, 76, 482–497.

Sheldon, K. M., and Houser-Marko, L. (2001). Self-Concordance, Goal Attainment, and the Pursuit of Happiness: Can There Be an Upward Spiral? *Journal of Personality and Social Psychology*, 80, 152–165.

Smiles, S. (1958). *Self-Help.* John Murray.

Smith, A. (1976). *The Theory of Moral Sentiments.* Oxford University Press.

Templeton, S. K. (2004). Happiness Is the New Economics. *Sunday Times*, December 5.

Tharp, T. (2005). *The Creative Habit: Learn It and Use It for Life.* Simon and Schuster.

Thoreau, H. D. (1995). *Walden; Or, Life in the Woods.* Dover Publications.

Watson, D. (2002). Positive Affectivity: The Disposition to Experience Pleasurable Emotional States. In C. R. Snyder and S. J. Lopez (eds.), *Handbook of Positive Psychology*, 106–119. Oxford University Press.

Williamson, M. (1996). *Return to Love: Reflections on the Principles of a Course in Miracles.* HarperCollins.

Wilson, J. Q. (1993). *The Moral Sense.* Free Press.

Wrzesniewski, A., and Dutton, J. E. (2001). Crafting a Job: Revisioning Employees as Active Crafters of Their Work. *Academy of Management Journal*, 26, 179–201.

Wrzesniewski, A., McCauley, C., Rozin, P., and Schwartz, B. (1997). Jobs, Careers, and Callings: People's Relations to Their Work. *Journal of Research in Personality*, 31, 21–33.

Yalom, I. D. (1998). *The Yalom Reader: Selections from the Work of a Master Therapist and Storyteller.* Edited by B. Yalom. Basic Books.

# Index

**EXCLUSIVE PREVIEW!**

# The Pursuit of PERFECT

*TAL BEN-SHAHAR, Ph.D.*

AVAILABLE SPRING 2009

# Part 1

# The Theory

# Prologue

Out of everything that I write or teach, the topic of perfectionism is closest to my heart and mind. My personal evolution—still ongoing—in dealing with perfectionism captures my progress toward becoming happier, more confident, and calmer, as well as more successful. Given that this is such a personally meaningful topic to me, it was not surprising that my students would often remark that my lectures on perfectionism were the most meaningful ones to them too. After all, as Carl Rogers wrote, "What is most personal is most general."

My hope is to make this book as personally meaningful to you as writing it has been for me and as the topic has been for my students. Throughout the book, I share many personal anecdotes; these supplement and bring to life the rigorous research and scientific evidence that form the foundation of this book.

My previous book, *Happier*, explored the question of happiness—the nature of happiness and the kind of action we can take to bring more of it into our lives. This book, though it can be read on its own, takes the idea from *Happier* to a deeper level, looking less at ways of *doing* things that would lead to happiness and more at ways of *being* that would enable happiness. Among other things, this book explores what I have come to see as the most significant internal barrier to happiness—the false, unrealistic belief that a happy life comprises an unbroken flow of positive emotions and a flawless stream of successes.

A full and fulfilling life inevitably comprises struggles, failures, and painful emotions; and the pressure to be "happy" all of the time, the expectation that some unpleasant experiences or feelings should be avoided, or can be avoided, merely increases unhappiness.

Like *Happier*, this book is also a workbook. There are exercises at the end of each chapter, and throughout the text there are Time-Ins—opportunities for reflection and hence for better assimilation of the material. The exercises and Time-Ins can be done alone, in pairs, or in groups; the book can provide material for book clubs interested in personal development, as well as for couples wishing to cultivate more intimacy in their relationship with each other.

# Introduction

**In the depth of winter, I finally learned that there was within me an invincible summer.**

—*Albert Camus*

It was mid-January. I saw nothing around me as I cut across Harvard Yard toward the austere psychology building on the other side of campus. Once there, I stood before my professor's closed door, barely registering the tingling sensation in my fingertips. I raised my eyes and scanned the ID numbers on the grade sheet, column by column, and then straight across the page, finding it difficult to see clearly what was in front of me. Once again, my anxiety had rendered me nearly blind.

My first two years of college had been unhappy. I always felt that the sword of Damocles was hanging over my head. What if I missed a crucial word during a lecture? What if I were caught off guard during a seminar? What if I didn't have a chance to proofread my paper for a third and final time? Any of these situations could lead to an imperfect performance, to failure, to the end of the possibility of becoming the kind of person and attaining the kind of life that I envisioned for myself.

That day, standing at my professor's door, one of my great fears materialized. I failed to get an A. I rushed back to my room and locked the door behind me.

Nobody likes to fail, but there is a difference between a *normal aversion to failure* and an *intense fear of failure*. Aversion to failure motivates us to take necessary precautions and to work harder to achieve success. Intense fear of failure, by contrast, often handicaps us, making us reject failure so vigorously that we cannot take the risks that are necessary for growth. This fear not only compromises our performance but also jeopardizes our overall psychological well-being.

Failure is an unavoidable part of any life, and it is a necessary part of a successful life. We learn to walk by falling, to talk by babbling, to shoot a basket by missing, and to color the inside of a square by scribbling outside of it. Those who intensely fear failing end up falling short of their potential. *We either learn to fail or we fail to learn.*

Ten years later I was eating lunch in the dining hall of Leverett House, one of Harvard's undergraduate dormitories. It was October, the fall semester was in progress, and most of the leaves outside the window had turned glaring orange, red, and yellow. The most interesting ones to me were those that still seemed to be struggling to let nature take its course and turn those brighter hues.

"May I join you?" asked Matt, a senior. I was startled and my mouth was full, so I nodded and smiled. "I hear you're teaching a class on happiness," Matt said as he sat down opposite me.

"That's right, it's about positive psychology," I responded, eager to tell him all about my new course. But before I could elaborate, Matt jumped in: "You know, my roommate Steve is taking your class, so you'd better watch out."

"Watch out? Why?" I asked, expecting him to divulge some dark secret about Steve.

"Because," he replied, "if I ever see you unhappy, I'm going to tell him."

Matt was clearly joking—or, at least half-joking. The assumption underlying his remark, though, was a serious—and a common—one: that a happy life is composed of a perfect stream of positive emotions, and that a person who experiences envy or anger, disappointment or sadness, fear or anxiety, is not *really* happy. But in fact, the only people who don't experience normal unpleasant feelings are psychopaths. And the dead. Experiencing these emotions, at times, is actually a good sign—a sign that we are most likely not psychopathic and most certainly alive.

Paradoxically, when we do not allow ourselves to experience painful emotions, we limit our capacity for happiness. All our feelings flow along the same emotional pipeline, so when we block painful emotions, we are also indirectly blocking pleasurable ones. And these painful emotions only expand and intensify when they aren't released. When they finally break through, and they eventually do break through in one way or another, they overwhelm us.

Painful emotions are an inevitable part of the experience of being human, and therefore rejecting them is ultimately rejecting part of our humanity. To lead a full and fulfilling life—a happy life—we need to allow ourselves to experience the full range of human emotions. In other words, *we need to give ourselves the permission to be human.*

Alasdair Clayre's life seemed perfect. He was a star student at Oxford University and later became one of its most celebrated scholars, winning accolades, awards, and fellowships. Not one to restrict himself to the ivory tower, he published a novel and a collection of poems, and he recorded two albums that included some of his own compositions. He then wrote, directed, produced, and presented *The Heart of the Dragon*—a twelve-part television series on China.

The series won an Emmy Award, but Clayre was not there to receive it. Shortly after having completed the series, at the age of forty-eight, Clayre committed suicide by jumping in front of a moving train.

Would knowing that he was about to win an Emmy have made any difference? His former wife says, "The Emmy was a symbol of success that would have meant a great deal to him, that would have given him self-esteem." But, she adds, "he had so many symbols of success much grander than the Emmy" and none of them had satisfied him; "he needed a new one each time he did something."[1]

Ultimately, Clayre never saw anything he did as good enough. Although he was clearly a great success, he was unable to see himself as successful. He actually rejected success. First, he consistently measured himself against standards that were almost impossible to meet; second, even when he attained the near impossible, he would quickly dismiss his success as trivial and move on to the next impossible dream.

The desire for success is part of our nature. And many of us are driven to reach greater and greater heights, something that can lead to personal success and societal progress. Great expectations can indeed lead to great rewards. To live a life that is both successful and fulfilling, though, our standards of success must be *realistic*, and we must be able to enjoy, and be grateful for, our achievements. *We need to ground our dreams and appreciate our accomplishments.*

These three stories—of my extreme fear of a less-than-perfect grade, of Matt's warning that I had better seem happy all the time, and of the tragedy of Clayre's inability to enjoy success—capture three distinct yet interrelated dimensions of perfectionism: rejection of *failure*, rejection of *painful emotions*, and rejection of *success*. We see the negative effects of these dimensions of perfectionism all around us and often within us.

We see intense fear of failure in schoolchildren who do not venture outside the box, who stop experimenting, and thus diminish their capacity to learn and grow; in college students who become chronic procrastinators, afraid to begin a project if they are not certain of a perfect outcome. We see it in the workplace, where innovation is sacrificed on the altar of the tried and true, the safe—and the mediocre.

Behaviors like these are not the *only* manifestations of intense fear of failure. Sometimes we turn this fear inward. We all know people who seem perennially cheerful even in the face of major disappointments, who are relentlessly optimistic regardless of objective reality, who bounce back quickly and seem emotionally unscathed following real traumas and tragedies. While of course a positive attitude and resilience contribute to well-being, rejecting painful emotions because there is no room for them in our idealized vision of a happy life is unhealthy in the long run. Taking emotional shortcuts—detouring to avoid certain feelings—can, paradoxically, diminish happiness.

It's easy to understand how perfectionism leads to the rejection of failure and painful emotions. What is more surprising, though, is how perfectionism can lead to the rejection of *success*. We see this in people who seem to "have it all" but remain unhappy. If the only dream we have is of a perfect life, we are doomed to disappointment because such a dream simply cannot come true in the real world. It was Clayre's intense perfectionism that made all of his real-life accomplishments seem trivial and made him unable to take real and lasting pleasure in his successes.

**TIME-IN** Can you recognize yourself or someone you know in one of the three stories?

For a long time perfectionism was understood by psychologists as a kind of neurosis. In 1981, psychologist David Burns described perfectionists as "those whose standards are high beyond reach or reason, people who strain compulsively and unremittingly toward impossible goals and who measure their own worth entirely in terms of productivity and accomplishment." Recently, psychologists have begun to see perfectionism as more complex and have begun to explore the ways in which it may not be purely negative. Indeed, they have found that perfectionism can be beneficial in some ways, driving people to work hard and set high personal standards.

Psychologists today differentiate between "positive perfectionism," which is adaptive and healthy, and "negative perfectionism," which is maladaptive and neurotic.[2] I actually see these two types of perfectionism as so dramatically different in both their underlying nature and their ramifications that I prefer to use entirely different terms to refer to them. Throughout this book, I will refer to "negative perfectionism" as simply *perfectionism* and to "positive perfectionism" as *optimalism*.[3]

The fundamental difference between the Perfectionist and the Optimalist is that the former essentially *rejects* reality while the latter *accepts* it. We can see this in the way each perceives and reacts to failure, painful emotions, and success.

The Perfectionist expects her path toward any goal to be direct, smooth, and free of obstacles. When, inevitably, it isn't—when, for instance, she fails at something—she is unable to cope. While the Perfectionist *rejects failure*, the Optimalist *accepts* it as a natural part of life and inextricably linked to success. I was unhappy throughout college, in large part because I could not accept failure as a necessary part of learning—and living.

The Perfectionist believes that a happy life comprises a perfect stream of positive emotions. And because he of course aspires to be happy, he *rejects* painful emotions. The Optimalist, on the other hand, *accepts* that painful emotions are an inevitable part of being alive. Matt, the student who threatened that he would tell his roommate if he saw me unhappy, thought a "happiness expert" should radiate joy 24/7. Matt's idea was not only *unrealistic*; it was in fact a recipe for *unhappiness*.

The Perfectionist is never satisfied. She consistently sets standards that are more or less impossible to meet, thereby *rejecting* the possibility of success from the outset. No matter what she achieves it never seems good enough to her, and she can never take any pleasure in her accomplishments. The Optimalist sets extremely high standards too, but standards that are nevertheless possible to meet because they are grounded in reality. In this regard, what differentiates the Optimalist from the Perfectionist is the Optimalist's *acceptance* of reality. When the Optimalist reaches her goals, she feels real satisfaction and real pleasure in her success. Clayre desperately chased success throughout his life, but because he held on to an impossible dream of what success would entail, he could never attain it and thus could never be happy.

Perfectionists *reject reality* and replace it with a *fantasy* world—a world in which there is no failure and no painful emotion and in which their standards for success, no matter how unrealistic, can actually be met. Optimalists *accept reality*—they accept that in the real world some failure and some sorrow are inevitable, and that success has to be measured against standards that are actually attainable.

Perfectionists pay a high emotional price for rejecting reality. Their rejection of failure leads to anxiety because the possibility that they might fail is always imminent. Their rejection of painful emotions often leads to an intensification of the very emotion they are trying to suppress, ultimately leading to even more pain. Their rejection of real-world limits and constraints leads them to set unreasonable and unattainable standards of success, and because they can never meet these standards, they are constantly plagued by feelings of frustration and inadequacy.

Optimalists gain great emotional benefit from accepting reality. Because they accept failure as natural—even if they don't *enjoy* failing—they experience less performance anxiety and derive more enjoyment from their activities. Because they accept painful emotions as an inevitable part of being alive, they do not exacerbate them by trying to suppress them—they experience them and move on. Because they accept real-world limits and constraints, they set goals that they actually can attain and are thus able to experience—and enjoy—success.

| **Perfectionist** | **Optimalist** |
|---|---|
| Rejects failure | Accepts failure |
| Rejects painful emotions | Accepts painful emotions |
| Rejects success | Accepts success |
| REJECTS REALITY | ACCEPTS REALITY |

To summarize, Perfectionists reject everything—emotions, achievements, themselves or other people—that deviates from their flawless, faultless ideal vision.

If her vision of the ideal life is one in which she always feels positive and fulfilled, she will see sadness or frustration as a threat to her sense of self and reject these feelings. Conversely, if she idealizes the life of the alienated, misunderstood outsider, the starving artist, or tormented genius, she will reject ordinary comforts, pleasures, and satisfactions. If she idealizes success, every setback or failure is a threat; if she has an image of her ideal relationship, any real-life partner will inevitably fall short of her expectations.

The Optimalist, by contrast, accepts reality and refuses to waste time, energy, and the potential to really enjoy her studies, work, and relationships by constantly fighting the facts of life. She may have ideas about what her ideal career, daily life, or relationship would look like, but she also understands that nothing in life is perfect—that painful emotions are a part of life; that failure and success are two sides of the same coin, and that true love is about two real, imperfect people getting together.

## Notes

1. Quoted in Blatt, 1995.
2. Hamachek 1978
3. I draw on the work of Hewitt and Flett (1991), as well as Frost (1990), who explain perfectionism as a multidimensional construct.